GOLDEN HART GUIDES

STRATFORD-UPON-AVON & THE COTSWOLDS

GOLDEN HART GUIDES

Stratford -upon- Avon & the Cotswolds

Catherine Dupre &
Caroline Hartnell

SIDGWICK & JACKSON LONDON
in association with Trusthouse Forte

Front cover photo: Holy Trinity Church
Stratford-upon-Avon
Back cover photo: Lower Slaughter
Frontispiece: Shakespeare's Birthplace

Photographs by the British Tourist
Authority, with the exception of
ps 8,11 Mansell Collection; 21
Paul Watkins; 47, 62 (bottom), 63
Dr John Wilson

Compiled and designed by Paul Watkins
Editorial associate: Anthony Edkins
Maps: John Flower

First published in Great Britain 1984
by Sidgwick & Jackson in association
with Trusthouse Forte

ISBN 0-283-98910-6

Photoset by Falcon Graphic Art Ltd,
Wallington, Surrey
Printed and bound in Great Britain
by Hazell Watson and Viney Limited,
Aylesbury, Bucks
for Sidgwick & Jackson Limited,
1 Tavistock Chambers, Bloomsbury Way,
London WC1A 2SG

Contents

Introduction

Despite the numerous books that have been written on the Cotswolds, the people who live in the region, those who write about it, and those who visit it, all have their view as to what area can most genuinely be called 'the Cotswolds'.

Topographically, it is the 100-mile ridge of hills that stretches from Chipping Campden in the north to Bath in the south-west. On the west, the hills drop dramatically – the Cotswold Edge or Scarp – into the plains of the Severn Valley, but on the east it is more difficult to define a border where the Cotswolds end and merge into the flatter countryside of Oxfordshire. Geologically there is a change in the region of Hook Norton and Great Rollright, for it is here that the pale grey Cotswold oolite stone gives way to the brown ironstone of Oxfordshire. It is this oolite limestone that gives the region its architectural character, for the Cotswold building, whether a cottage, barn, manor house or church is built of this soft grey-yellow stone, and tiled with stone from the local quarries of Burford and Stonesfield.

Before the Saxons, the area had been inhabited for at least 3000 years: the monuments of the Stone Age peoples – Belas Knap, the Rollright Stones and others – are a part of the upland scenery. Later on the Romans left their mark, building the roads and settlements that became the basis of the trading routes and wool towns of the Middle Ages.

Wool and the Cotswolds are inseparable; the wealth generated by the trade created many of the region's finest towns – Stroud, Painswick, Chipping Campden – and many of its splendid churches. It did much, too, to maintain the style of the great landed families – the Forteys of Northleach, the Fettiplaces of Swinbrook – whose estates imposed further order on the landscape, leaving a heritage of fine buildings.

The suppression of the wool trade by the Enclosure Acts brought decline to the Cotswolds in the 19th century, but in the 20th century the tourist trade brought new life to the area, and this has at least preserved something of the charm of the Cotswolds. Sometimes, in villages such as Bourton-on-the-Water, the price seems too high. Here the original village is submerged beneath a confusion of gift shops, cafés and museums. Yet other villages, equally popular with the tourist, such as Bibury, Burford or Chipping Campden, have managed to keep their charm and identity.

Saddest of all is the small village that, charming as it is, has not enough to attract the tourist, and is now a community of retired people. No longer is there the clump and clatter of the farm wagons as they trundle through the village street, or the noisy children coming out of school, or, in the evenings, farm labourers returning from the fields with their dogs. Now these villages are silent places: they have no shop, no pub, no school.

Tractors and mechanical cultivators have replaced the wagon and horses; one man will run a farm that used to employ a dozen labourers. The village church will probably be one of a group sharing a single priest, with a small congregation. The burden of supporting these important buildings now rests on small communities or organisations such as the Historic Churches Preservation Trust, for it is essential that these small villages, with their churches and manor houses, be preserved for the enjoyment of future generations.

Within easy reach of the Cotswolds – only 12 miles north of Chipping Campden – is Stratford-upon-Avon. The birthplace of William Shakespeare, this is a pilgrimage place for visitors from all over the world. Perfectly sited on the banks of the Avon in the midst of Warwickshire's meadowland, it retains its market-town character and many buildings of Shakespeare's period.

In addition to Stratford and the major towns of the Cotswolds, such as Cheltenham and Cirencester, which are of obvious interest and importance, this short book endeavours to draw the visitor's attention to some of the lesser known places. Inevitably there will be those who will question the choice and feel that a particular village should have been included, or another left out: no book can claim to be more than an introduction to an area so rich in natural beauty and historical interest. Once the visitor to the Cotswolds has felt its magic he will want to explore the region for himself and make it more truly his own.

The Cotswolds

A Brief History

Prehistory Many early communities colonised the Cotswolds in prehistoric times, leaving traces of their occupation in a number of primitive sites. In the north-east are the mysterious Rollright Stones, some set in a circle and others, the Whispering Knights, forming a burial chamber. These stones have long been the object of local superstition. According to Stukely, the 18th-century antiquarian, on Midsummer Eve the village maidens would go one by one to the Knights in the hope of hearing in their whispering what their own fate was to be. In the south-west are the Stone Age burial mounds, or long barrows: Belas Knap on Cleeve Common and Hetty Pegler's Tump near Uley. Iron Age hill forts abound: the most impressive is at Uleybury.

The Romans did much to shape the modern Cotswolds, building many of the roads that are now in use. The great Foss (or Fosse) Way ran in a straight line from Moreton-in-Marsh to Bath, and on it the Romans established the important town of Corinium (modern Cirencester). The Foss was originally a frontier rather than a road, stretching across England from Exeter to Lincoln, with its axis at Corinium. The site was presumably chosen because of its proximity to Bagendon, the chief town of the early British Dobunni tribe, who were friendly to the Roman conquerors. Although Corinium was burnt to the ground by the Saxons in the 6th century, the site of the large amphitheatre outside the town, and remains of the enormous fortified city walls, have enabled scholars to make reconstructions of

Tetbury in the early 19th century

the Roman town. Remains of several Roman villas have been excavated in the Cotswolds; the most interesting at Woodchester and Chedworth.

Medieval wool towns After the Romans the Foss continued to be used as a trade route, and the Roman market towns evolved into the medieval markets of Stow-on-the-Wold, Moreton-in-Marsh and Northleach. During the 12th century the Cotswolds became one of the most important wool trading areas in Europe, and merchants from London and the Continent made their way up the Foss to buy wool, at first mainly for export. The Italians called the Cotswolds 'Chondisgualdo' and Northleach 'Norleccio'.

More and more of the great Cotswold sheep (a breed now almost extinct, but still to be seen at the Cotswold Farm Park at Guiting Power) roamed the hillsides. 'Upon these hills are fed large flocks of sheep with the whitest wool, having long necks and square bodies', Camden wrote in his *Britannia*. Wool was to be the region's main source of wealth and prosperity until the 17th century. The wool merchants became rich men, and it was their money that built the great wool churches at Cirencester, Chipping Campden, Burford, Northleach and Fairford, and the splendid merchants' houses at Chipping Campden, Painswick and Burford.

Modest Norman and Early English churches were increased in size and grandeur: the naves were heightened, usually with a clerestory, towers were added, chancels were rebuilt. Then, when their

time came, these merchant benefactors were laid to rest in tombs of suitable magnificence. Northleach has particularly fine memorial brasses: Thomas and John Fortey lie there, the father and son who were responsible for rebuilding the church. Their Tudor house still stands in the village, with the emblem of the Fortey family on the gateway through which the wool wagons would have been driven. The wool trade of Northleach is particularly well recorded, for it was here that the Cely family, Richard and his three sons, did much of their business: an account of their lives is recorded in *The Cely Papers* (1475-88).

The Dissolution of the Monasteries, which took place under Henry VIII had many important economic consequences, causing a major redistribution of wealth and an alteration to the pattern of patronage. Towns with great abbeys, such as Winchcombe, which had been dependent on the trade generated by pilgrims, were suddenly deprived of their livelihood, and the importance of wool as a source of revenue was enhanced.

The great builders The wool provided the money, and the stone provided the building material: for centuries these two natural products kept the Cotswolds prosperous. The stone and the masons who worked it brought further wealth to the region. Their stone was to be used in many important buildings: in the colleges of Oxford; at Eton and Windsor, in the school and for St George's Chapel; for the rebuilding of London after the Great Fire; for Sir Christopher Wren's great cathedral, St Paul's. Often the master masons went with their stone: Thomas and Edward Strong worked for Wren on the Sheldonian Theatre at Oxford and then in London on the City churches. On a memorial tablet in Burford church Christopher Kempster, a local mason, is remembered for his work on St Paul's.

But the greatest memorial to these men are the buildings that can be seen everywhere in the Cotswold Hills. Villages and churches, cottages and mansions, a countryside that has been developed and enriched with the stone from its quarries and by the work of its own craftsmen.

Decline of the land By the early 17th century the prosperity of the Cotswolds was beginning to decline. Gloucestershire sheep had been exported to the Continent, mainly to Spain. Here they were crossed with Spanish breeds, and a new and stronger wool was being produced. Lancashire mills were beginning to produce cotton. The price of wool dropped dramatically – the great days of wool wealth were over.

As the century proceeded, the pressure on farmers to produce more corn and arable crops led to the enclosure movement. From 1795 to 1812 over 1500 Enclosure Acts were passed. This was death to the small yeoman farmer: it was also the end of the great sheep runs over the Cotswold hills. This was the period when the drystone walls were built – such a feature of the Cotswold landscape today. Stone was still cheap and plentiful, as was the labour to work it. 'The price of New Dry Walling on Guiting Hill is Sixteen pence per Perch 4ft high'

James Agg noted in his diary for 1798. These walls were both quicker to erect and cheaper to maintain than the hedges which are used more commonly in other parts of the country. This, of course, is no longer the case, and today many walls have fallen into disrepair, the labour to rebuild them being both scarce and expensive.

Without the wool industry there was little alternative work, and poverty became a major social problem. The discontent and misery of the people blazed up in the Swing Riots of 1831, when threshing machines were destroyed, particularly in the Tetbury, Fairford and Chipping Norton districts. The threshing machine symbolised to the peasantry the replacement of sheep by corn.

Industrial growth The Stroud Valley has to be seen as a separate entity, and the decline of its fortunes came later. In many respects this area differs completely from the quiet wolds, with their history of sheep farming and stone quarrying. The country is more dramatic, steep hills dropping into the wooded valleys of the many streams that were used to work the cloth mills. By the 17th century Stroud had become an industrial rather than an agricultural community: in 1608 it is recorded that half the population of the villages in the area were employed in some capacity in the cloth industry. There were spinners, weavers and dyers, and much of their work was carried out in the cottages. The cloth manufactured at Stroud was a fine, expensive material: most famous was the red and blue cloth made for the army. By the early

Bourton-on-the-Hill

part of the 19th century there were 150 mills operating in the Stroud area. Like the stonemasons and wool merchants of the 'wool' towns, the clothiers are commemorated by tombs and monuments in the local churches.

Cottage vs factory Unfortunately, the determination of the cottagers to keep as much work as possible in their own cottages prevented the introduction of more sophisticated machinery. And the attempt to compete resulted in pressure to hold down wages, so that workers and their families were often near to starvation. A strike of the weavers of Stroud for better conditions was put down by the army under the leadership of James Wolfe (the future General Wolfe of Quebec). By 1825 the demand for the expensive cloth produced in the area had declined so dramatically that even

the wealthiest clothiers, such as Edward Sheppard of Uley, went bankrupt.

Some parts of the Cotswolds found an alternative means of livelihood: Burford, for instance, had a thriving coaching trade, with sometimes as many as 40 stage coaches a day passing through the town on their way to and from London. In the south-west, the proximity to Bristol of such towns as Dursley and Wotton-under-Edge ensured their survival: elsewhere the Cotswolds returned to their agricultural roots.

But ultimately it is the tourist industry that has saved the Cotswolds. The little villages and hamlets, dotted about the hillsides, every year attract more visitors from all parts of the world. Here they can find the peace and charm of a way of life that has almost vanished.

The Best of the Region

excluding Stratford-upon-Avon (p.22)

A summary of the places of interest in the region, open to the public. The location, with map reference, is shown in the Gazetteer. Names in bold are Gazetteer entries, and those with an asterisk are considered to be of outstanding interest. (NT) indicates properties owned by the National Trust

All Saints, North Cerney

Churches

Those listed here are specially worth a visit, either for the building itself, or for some special feature such as brasses, heraldry, tomb or wall-painting.

Beverston St Mary

Bibury St Mary

Bishop's Cleeve St Michael & All Angels

Bisley All Saints

* **Bledington** St Leonard

Blockley St Peter & St Paul

Buckland St Michael

* **Burford** St John the Baptist

Cheltenham St Mary

* **Chipping Campden** St James

Chipping Norton St Mary's

* **Cirencester** St John the Baptist

Coberley St Giles

Daglingworth Holy Rood

Duntisbourne Rouse St Michael

Elkstone St John

* **Fairford** St Mary

Great Barrington St Mary

Hailes Church

Hatherop St Nicholas

Kempsford St Mary the Virgin

Lechlade St Lawrence

Leonard Stanley St Swithin

Longborough St James

Minchinhampton Holy Trinity

* **North Cerney** All Saints

* **Northleach** St Peter & St Paul

Oddington St Nicholas

Owlpen Holy Cross

Painswick St Mary

Rendcomb St Peter

* **Sapperton** St Kenelm

Selsley All Saints

Southrop St Peter

STRATFORD-UPON-AVON (p 24)

Swinbrook St Mary

Tetbury St Mary

* Winchcombe St Peter

Wotton-under-Edge St Mary the Virgin

Historic Houses

Admission to most historic houses is between £1-2 (children half-price).

Beverston Castle
Written enquiry only

Buckland Rectory
May-Jul & Sep, Mon 11-4. Aug, Mon & Fri 11-4

Burford Priory
By appointment

Charlecote Park (NT)
Apr & Oct, Sat, Sun & Easter week 11-5. May-Sep, daily except Mon (open Bank Hols) 11-6

* **Chastleton House**
Fri-Sun & Bank Hols 2-5. Confirm: Tel (060874) 355

* **Chavenage House**
May-Sep, Thur, Sun & Bank Hols 2-6

* **Cheltenham** Pittville Pump Room
Daily 8-5

Compton Wynyates
Closed to the public, but see Gazetteer

Honington Hall
May-Sep, Wed, Thur & Bank Hol Mons 2.30-5.30

Kelmscott Manor
Apr-Sep, 1st Wed in month 11-1 & 2-5

Minchinhampton Market House
Sat, Sun & Bank Hols 9-5.30 by appointment

Owlpen Manor
Written enquiry only

Painswick Court House
Jun-Sep, Thur 2-5 by appointment

Painswick House
Jul-Sep, Sat & Sun 2-6

Sapperton Daneway House
Written enquiry only

Sezincote
May-Jul & Sep, Thur & Fri 2.30-6

Snowshill Manor (NT)
May-Sep, Wed-Sun & Bank Hols 11-1 & 2-6. Apr-Oct, Sat, Sun & Bank Hols 11-1 & 2-6

STRATFORD-UPON-AVON (p 24)

* **Sudeley Castle**
Mar-Oct, daily 12-5.30. Gardens 11-6

Upper Slaughter Manor House
May-Sep, Fri 2-5.30

Upton House (NT)
Apr-Sep, Mon-Thur; also weekends in early May & Aug 2-6

Parks, Gardens & Wildlife
(see also *Nature Trails*, p.18)

Admission to the gardens of historic houses is usually included in a combined ticket for house and garden. (See admission to historic houses above.) Where the garden can be visited separately this is usually about half the price of the combined ticket. The entrance fee for other gardens open to the public is usually in the range 30-50p (Children half-price or less).

Barnsley House Gardens
Wed 10-6 (or dusk). 1st Sun in May, Jun & July 2-7. Otherwise by appointment

* **Batsford Park Arboretum**
Apr-Oct, daily 10-5

Bibury Trout Farm
Mar-Dec, daily 1-6 (or dusk)

* **Bourton-on-the-Water** Birdland
Mar-Nov, daily 10-6; Dec-Feb, daily 10.30-4

Bourton-on-the-Water Windrush Trout Farm
Apr-Oct, daily 10.30-5.30; Nov-Mar, 11-4

* **Burford** Cotswold Wildlife Park
Daily 10-6 (or dusk)

Charlecote Park (NT)
House & park. See *Historic Houses*

Cirencester Park
Daily

Guiting Power Cotswold Farm Park
See *Industrial & Rural Heritage*

* **Hidcote Manor** (NT)
Apr-Oct, daily (not Tue & Fri) 11-8

* **Kiftsgate Court**
Apr-Sep, Wed, Thur, Sun & Bank
Hols 2-6

Miserden Misarden Park
Easter-Oct, Wed & Thur 10-4.30

Prinknash Abbey Bird Park
Mar-Oct, daily 10-6; Nov-Feb, Sat
& Sun 11-4 (or 1hr before dusk)

Rodmarton Manor
Jun-Aug, Thur 2-6

Sezincote
Thur, Fri & Bank Hols 2-6. Closed
Dec

Stanway House
Jun-Aug, Wed & Sun 2-6

Sudeley Castle
House & park. See *Historic Houses*

Upper Swell Abbotswood
Some Suns in spring & early
summer

Upper Swell Donnington Fish Farm
Mon-Fri 9-7, Sat & Sun 10-6

Upton House (NT)
House & garden. See *Historic Houses*

* **Westonbirt Arboretum**
Daily 10-8 (or dusk)

Castles, Ruins & Ancient Sites

Unless otherwise stated, these sites
are accessible at all reasonable times.

Bagendon Dykes
Iron Age ditches

* **Belas Knap**
Neolithic burial mound

* **Chedworth Roman Villa** (NT)
Mar-Oct, Tue-Sun & Bank Hols 11-
6 (closed Good Fri); Nov, Dec &
Feb, Wed-Sun 11-4

Crickley Hill Country Park
Excavation of hill fort, 6 weeks in
summer

Great Witcombe Witcombe Roman
Villa

* **Hailes Abbey** (NT)
Mid-Mar to mid-Oct, Mon-Sat 9.30-
6.30, Sun 2-6.30; mid-Oct to mid-
Mar, Mon-Sat 9.30-4, Sun 2-4

Notgrove Long Barrow
Prehistoric tomb

Rollright Stones
Prehistoric monoliths

Uley Uleybury Camp
Iron Age hill fort

Uley Hetty Pegler's Tump
Neolithic burial mound

* **Wotton-under-Edge** Wotton Mosaic
Reconstruction of Woodchester
Roman Pavement

Museums & Galleries

Bibury Arlington Mill
See *Industrial & Rural Heritage*

Bourton-on-the-Water Motor
Museum
Feb-Nov, daily 10-6

Burford Tolsey House Museum
Easter-Sep, daily 2.30-5.30. Guided
tours of the town from the museum
May-Oct, Sun 3pm. Jul & Aug, Sun
& Wed 3pm

* **Cheltenham** Art Gallery & Museum
Mon-Sat 10-5.30. Closed Bank Hols

Cheltenham Holst Birthplace
Museum
Tue-Fri 12-5.30; Sat 11-5.30. Closed
Bank Hols

* **Cheltenham** Pittville Pump Room
Museum
Apr-Oct, Tue-Sun 10.30-5; Nov-
Mar, Tue-Sat 10.30-5. Closed Bank
Hols

Chipping Campden Campden Car
Collection
Easter, May-Sep daily 11-6

Chipping Campden Woolstaplers'
Hall Museum
Easter, May-Sep daily 11-6

Cirencester Corinium Museum
May-Sep, Mon-Sat 10-6, Sun 2-6.
Oct-Apr, Tue-Sat 10-5, Sun 2-5

Cirencester (Kemble) Smerrill Farm
Museum
See *Industrial & Rural Heritage*

Hailes Abbey Museum
See *Castles, Ruins & Ancient Sites*

Moreton-in-Marsh (Aston Magna)
Bygones Museum, Bank Farm
See *Industrial & Rural Heritage*

Northleach Cotswold Countryside
Collection
See *Industrial & Rural Heritage*

Snowshill Manor Museum
See *Historic Houses*

STRATFORD-UPON-AVON (p.24)

Stroud Museum
Mon-Sat 10.30-1, 2-5. Closed Bank
Hols

Stroud Subscription Rooms
Mon-Sat 10-5. Closed Bank Hols

Sudeley Castle Museum
See *Historic Houses*

Tetbury Police Museum
Easter Mon-end Oct, daily 10.15-
4.30

Winchcombe Railway Museum
See *Industrial & Rural Heritage*

Winchcombe (Toddington) GWR
Exhibition
See *Industrial & Rural Heritage*

Wotton-under-Edge Wotton Mosaic
See *Castles, Ruins & Ancient Sites*

Industrial & Rural Heritage

* **Bibury** Arlington Mill
Mar-Oct, daily 10.30-7 (or dusk);
Nov-Feb, weekends only

Bourton-on-the-Hill Tithe Barn

Cirencester (Kemble) Smerrill Farm
Museum
Daily 10.30-6. Closed Dec 24-26

Coates
Entrance to Thames-Severn Canal
tunnel

Donnington Brewery
Appointment only

* **Guiting Power** Cotswold Farm
Park
May-Sep, daily 10.30-6

Moreton-in-Marsh (Aston Magna)
Bygones Museum, Bank Farm
Easter-Oct, Wed & Bank Hols 10.30-
6, Sun 11-6. Otherwise by
appointment

* **Northleach** Cotswold Countryside
Collection
May-Sep, Mon-Sat 10-6, Sun 2-6

* **Stinchcombe** Cider Mill Gallery,
Blanchworth Farm
Cider-making with horse-drawn mill
and press. Jun-Aug, Tue-Sun 11-5;
Sep-Dec, Apr & May, Tue-Sat 11-5

Winchcombe Railway Museum
Easter, Bank Hols, Sun & Mon 2.30-
6; 1st week in Aug, daily 2.30-6

Winchcombe (Toddington) GWR
Exhibition
Daily

Crafts & Local Interest

Normal shopping hours apply to
premises unless otherwise shown.

Bourton-on-the-Water Cotswold
Perfumery
Perfumes made on the premises.

Chipping Campden Campden
Pottery

Cirencester Cirencester Workshops
11 independent craft workshops,
exhibition gallery and shop

Prinknash Abbey Pottery
Pottery workshops Mon-Sat 10-12.30
& 1.30-5. Pottery shop daily 9-6

Stinchcombe Cider Mill Gallery
See *Industrial & Rural Heritage*

Winchcombe Pottery

Brass Rubbing *Cirencester* Replica
brasses can be rubbed at the Tourist
Information Office, Mon-Fri 10-4.
Also brasses in the church: contact
Rev Lewis, Tel (0285) 3142.
Northleach Church: contact Post
Office or Tudor House, the Green.
Wotton-under-Edge Replicas of the
Berkeley brasses can be rubbed
opposite S porch of church.

Famous Connections

Many famous names have Cotswolds connections. Details of their association will be found under the Gazetteer entries.

Austen, Jane Adlestrop

Butler, Lord R.A. Minchinhampton, Gatcombe Park

Charles I Sudeley Castle

Elizabeth I Sudeley Castle

Hastings, Warren Daylesford

Holst, Gustav Cheltenham, Wyck Rissington

Jenner, Edward Wotton-under-Edge

Keble, John Coln St Aldwyns, Eastleach Martin, Fairford, Southrop

Lee, Laurie Stroud, Slad

Lenthall, Speaker William Burford

Mitford, Nancy & Unity Asthall, Batsford, Swinbrook

Parr, Catherine Sudeley Castle

Pitman, Isaac Wotton-under-Edge

Prince & Princess of Wales Tetbury, Highgrove House

Prince & Princess Michael of Kent Stroud, Nether Lypiatt Manor

Princess Anne Minchinhampton, Gatcombe Park

Ricardo, David Minchinhampton, Gatcombe Park

Seymour, Thomas Sudeley Castle

Shelley, Percy B. Lechlade

Thomas, Edward Adlestrop

Vaughan Williams, Ralph Down Ampney

Whittington, Dick Coberley

Wilson, Edward Cheltenham, Leckhampton

Hotels & Historic Inns

(THF) A Trusthouse Forte Hotel

Broadway
The Lygon Arms
High Street, Broadway WR12 7DU
Tel (0386) 852255
Formerly a manor house and one of Broadway's finest period buildings, *The Lygon Arms* has welcomed travellers since the 16th c. On separate occasions during the Civil War, both Charles I and Cromwell took refuge here. Traditional hospitality is offered in a setting of antique furniture, inglenook fireplaces and oaken beams.

Burford
Lamb Inn
Sheep Street, Burford OX8 4LR
Tel (099382) 3155
This fine 15th-c. house was not recorded as an inn until the 18th c. The hotel has been in the same family for two generations and retains its beautiful antique furniture. With its open fires surrounded by oak settles, it is hard to realise that *The Lamb* functions as a modern hotel, with all the amenities. These include an excellent restaurant and good bar food in the middle of the day.

Cheltenham
The Queen's Hotel (THF)
Promenade, Cheltenham GL50 1NN
Tel (0242) 514724
This magnificent white stucco building, designed by the Cheltenham architect R.W. Jearrad in 1838, is a replica of the Temple of Jupiter in Rome. With its fine five-bay portico of Corinthian pillars and crowning pediment, the hotel dominates the classical Promenade, part of the town's early 19th-c. development as a fashionable spa.

Chipping Campden
The Cotswold House Hotel
High Street, Chipping Campden GL55 6AN
Tel (0386) 840330
This country hotel occupies two stone buildings in a typically-Cotswold combination of styles. The earlier may date from the 17th c., and its

neighbour, an early 19th-c. town house, has an elegant Adam-style staircase. Old beams and open fires make a warm welcome in winter, and the walled garden is open in the summer.

Chipping Norton
The White Hart Hotel (THF)
High Street, Chipping Norton
OX7 4AD
Tel (0608) 2572
A traditional coaching inn overlooking the market place. The mellow stone frontage is an 1811 addition to a Tudor building, part of which remains, but the inn may have medieval origins. A painted wall sign bears Richard II's badge. Inside there is period furniture from the 18th c., when *The White Hart* was a staging post.

Moreton-in-Marsh
The White Hart Royal (THF)
High Street, Moreton-in-Marsh
GL56 0BA
Tel (0608) 50731
This 16th-c. Cotswold-stone building was once half-timbered, and the arched entrance was used by horses in posting days. The interior has moulded ceiling beams, a fine open hearth and an interesting balustered staircase. Charles I slept here on a journey from Oxford to Evesham.

Painswick
The Falcon Hotel
Painswick GL6 6UN
Tel (0452) 812189
Built as an inn *c.* 1500 *The Falcon* was visited by Henry VIII when this was hunting country, and later served as a stage coach terminus. The old stables, retaining their original beams and horse trough, now house the Stable Bar. The bowling green, first laid out in 1560, is said to be the oldest in England.

Sport & Recreation

Fishing The Cotswold streams are famous for their trout fishing – Bibury and Fairford in particular are favourite spots for anglers. All fishing in the Cotswolds is either privately owned or in club hands, but permits can sometimes be obtained through a hotel or local sports shop. The Lechlade Trout Lodge offers angling facilities for an admission fee. There is also good coarse fishing at the Cotswold Water Park.

Water Sports 5m S of Cirencester, and signposted off the A419 to Swindon, is the Cotswold Water Park, where gravel workings have created almost 100 lakes. Although most activities are organized on a club basis, day tickets are available for windsurfing, angling and sailing. For further information ring Cirencester (0285) 861459.

Golf There are golf courses all over the area, and most accept visitors. Those at Minchinhampton Common and Cleeve Common are especially attractive.

Equestrian events There is steeple-chase racing in Cheltenham from Oct-May, including the Gold Cup meeting in March, and Cheltenham Horse Show is held in July. There are polo matches at Cirencester Park every Sunday in summer.

Festivals & Events

May *Cooper's Hill* Cheese-rolling ceremony; *Tetbury* Woolsack Races; *Dover's Hill, Chipping Campden* Dover's Games & Scuttlebrook Wake Fair (Fri & Sat after Spring Bank Hol Mon); *Bisley* Dressing of the Wells (Ascension Day)

June *Burford* Burford Dragon Procession (Midsummer's Eve)

July *Cheltenham* International Festival of Music (1st fortnight), Cheltenham Horse Show; *Cirencester* Carnival (1st Sat); *Stroud* Stroud Show including International Brick & Rolling Pin Throwing Contest (2nd Sat)

August *Cheltenham* Cricket Festival; *Painswick* Guild of Gloucestershire Craftsmen Exhibition & Market (1st 3 weeks), Painswick Country Show (2nd Sat); *Cranham* Feast & Ox Roast (2nd weekend); *Bourton-on-the-Water* Water Game (Bank Hol Mon)

September *Moreton-in-Marsh*
Moreton-in-Marsh Show (1st Sat);
Painswick Clipping Service (Sat
nearest 19th)

October *Cheltenham* Festival of
Music, Speech, Drama & Dancing;
Stroud Festival of Religious Drama
& the Arts

Walks

There is an unlimited number of walks
in the Cotswolds – an area of
outstanding beauty criss-crossed by
hundreds of miles of footpath. Those
listed below are simply a selection.
All are circular and can be undertaken
without difficulty in half a day.
However, none should be embarked
upon without the relevant 1:50,000
OS map and a good pair of boots. In
addition to these walks the commons
in the W Cotswolds (particularly
Cleeve Common, Minchinhampton
Common and Rodborough Common)
and Cirencester Park are good walking
areas.

The Cotswold Way
Special mention should be made of
this long-distance footpath from Bath
to Chipping Campden, covering 97m.
It follows a route suggested by the
Ramblers' Association, which makes
use of the existing rights of way, and
the whole route is marked with the
symbol of an arrow below a white
dot. Following the edge of the
Cotswold Scarp for much of the time,
with dramatic views of the scenery
below, it takes in the highest point
of the Cotswolds at Cleeve Common
and numerous prehistoric sites,
including Belas Knap and Hetty
Pegler's Tump. Always near to roads
and villages, it makes easy and
enjoyable walking for walkers of all
abilities at any time of year. A useful
introduction to the Cotswold Way is
The Cotswold Way Handbook, available
from the Ramblers' Association. This
has a description of the route and
details of accommodation, inns etc.
More comprehensive in their
treatment are: *The Cotswold Way, a
Walker's Guide*, by Mark Richards

(Thornhill Press, Cheltenham), and
A Guide to the Cotswold Way, by
Richard Sale (Constable).

Other Publications There are numerous
publications on walking in the
Cotswolds, but once you know where
you are going the best idea is to contact
either the Ramblers' Association, c/o
R.A. Long, 27 Lambert Avenue,
Shurdington, Cheltenham, Tel (0242)
862594 or the Cotswold Wardens, c/o
County Planning Dept, Shire Hall,
Gloucester, Tel (0452) 21444 x 7542.
Both will give information about walks
in the area and both organise guided
walks.

Nature trails

There are also various marked walks
in the Cotswold area:
Broadway Tower Country Park Nature
walks Easter-Sep, 10-6
Chedworth Denfurlong Farm Trail
Chipping Campden Dover's Hill
Nature Trail
Cirencester Park Forestry and farm
trails
Cooper's Hill Longest nature trail in
the Cotswolds
Crickley Hill Country Park Ecology,
geology and archaeology trails, and a
family trail suitable for disabled people
and people with pushchairs
Guiting Power Cotswold Farm Park
Farm Trail
Leckhampton Hill Walk

Walk 1 *Burford to Asthall*
Leave Burford on the old Witney
Road. In 1½m at Widford Mill turn
left over bridge. Take footpath to right
over fields towards Swinbrook,
passing St Oswald's Church and
terraces of the vanished Swinbrook
House, home of the Fettiplaces. Past
Swinbrook church, turn right onto
the road. Follow Z-bend towards
Swan Inn on the river. Before the
pub, take footpath left leading on N
side of the river to Asthall (½m). On
reaching the road turn right and
proceed through the village, returning
to Widford by road and back to
Burford/5m

Walk 2 *Southrop to the Eastleaches*
From *Swan Inn*, Southrop, take road
to Eastleach Turville. In 150 yds a
footpath leads right across a field.
After 150yds bear N to Eastleach
Turville (1m). At village bear right
along road to clapper bridge. Cross
it into Eastleach Martin, through the
churchyard and on to road to
Southrop/4m

Walk 3 *Lechlade Riverside Walk*
From Lechlade churchyard, follow
hard path E ½m. Cross main road
(A417) into junction road B4449.
Follow this road 200yds and turn right
down broad path leading to riverside
meadows. Follow River Thames E to
Buscot Weir. Cross to S bank of river
and sharp right through gate to Buscot
church. Rejoin A417 and follow ½m
to St John's Bridge (do not cross).
Follow footpath beside lock and return
on S side of river to Lechlade/3½m

Walk 4 *Bourton-on-the-Water to the*
Slaughters
Cross A429 near public house NW of
Bourton and take footpath opposite to
Lower Slaughter. In the village follow
the river left to the old mill (now the
post office) take footpath NW along
N bank of river to Upper Slaughter.
In the field before the village turn right
through the gate onto the road. Turn
left downhill and follow no through
road leading over ford and up to the
church. Return by road to Lower
Slaughter/3m

Walk 5 *Guiting Wood*
Take road NW from Guiting Power.
At cross-roads in 1m, turn right and
follow sign to small car park. Follow
narrow road NW along valley through
woods by river. In ¾m at junction
turn left and follow road ¾m W. A
footpath leads left from here on to
the edge of the wood. Follow this 1m
to the road, then follow road 2m back
to the car park or 2½m to Guiting
Power/5½/6m

Devil's Chimney, Leckhampton

Walk 6 *Leckhampton Hill*
At Seven Springs junction on A435/ A436 a narrow road leads NW (easy to miss but signposted to Cotswold Way). In ½m keep ahead and then leave road and follow signs along the Cotswold Way, which leads W along scarp overlooking Cheltenham. In 1m follow one of choice of paths around Leckhampton Hill, passing Iron Age fort (the edge is marked here by a trig. point). The Devil's Chimney is a clearly signposted detour. The Cotswold Way bears S, descending sharply to road. Turn left and follow 2m to starting point/5m

Walk 7 *Coates Canal Walk*
From Coates church a footpath leads SW ½m to the railway. Cross the railway to *The Tunnel House Inn*, with the monumental entrance to the old canal tunnel below. From here a footpath on the W bank of the canal leads S along the course of the canal to the road. On the S side of the road bridge the footpath leads back under the railway line. In ½m near Trewsbury House is a canal bridge. A detour S (½m) leads to the source of the River Thames. Going N of the canal bridge the footpath joins the road into Coates/2½m

Motoring Tours

The tours are circular and can be started at any point. A full day should be allowed for each tour.

Tour 1 *S Cotswolds Wool Churches*
Starting at Cirencester, the cathedral of the wool churches, leave by A417 to Fairford, where the church has medieval glass and monumental brasses. Turn back on road to Cirencester, and at W end of village turn right for Quenington, Coln St Aldwyns and Bibury. At junction with A433 Bibury church with its Saxon details is reached by a lane immediately left. Following A433 to Burford, see the splendid, originally Norman church. From Burford take A40 to Northleach, whose church has many fine brasses and monuments to wool merchants. At crossroads (A40 and A429, Foss Way) turn left for Cirencester and in ½m right, following directions to Chedworth (detour right, in 2m, to Chedworth Roman Villa). Go through village and then take left at junction for Cirencester. In 3m turn right for N Cerney with its attractive church. Follow A435 to Cirencester.

Tour 2 *N Cotswolds Gardens and Beauty Spots*
Leave Cheltenham by A46 for Winchcombe. In 2m at Cleeve Hill, Cleeve Common offers fine walks and splendid views. From Winchcombe take A46 for Broadway (detour right, in 2m, to Hailes Abbey). Leave Broadway on A44 for Chipping Norton. After 1m a right turn leads to a fine view from Broadway Hill. Continuing on A44 a left turn in 3m (B4081) leads to Chipping Campden. Going through village bear left on B4035. A side road to Dover's Hill, another good viewpoint, is shortly on left. Immediately after this take right (B4081) for Mickleton. The road goes under the railway: ½m further on turn right at crossroads to Hidcote Manor Gardens. From Hidcote follow directions to Ebrington and continue through village on B4035. In 3m turn right at junction with A429 for Moreton-in-Marsh. Just short of town turn right after railway bridge to Batsford village and Arboretum. From Moreton-in-Marsh continue on A429 through Stow-on-the-Wold and Bourton-on-the-Water to Northleach, then turn right on A40 and return to Cheltenham.

Tour 3 *Stratford-upon-Avon and Charlecote Park*
Leave Stratford by A34 (Oxford). 1m after Tredington turn left for Honington (Honington Hall). 1m S of village, take minor road for Upper Tysoe and after 4m turn right for Compton Wynyates. Continue on Upper Tysoe road through village to join A422. Turn right (Banbury) and in 2m left for Upton House. Back on A422 return towards Stratford and after Ettington, turn right on A429 to Wellesbourne. Left in village to Charlecote Park. Return to Stratford via B4086.

Coates canal tunnel

Stratford-upon-Avon

Population 99,400

Tourist Information 1 High Street Tel (0789) 293127. Summer, Mon-Sat 9-5.30, Sun 2-5; Winter 11-4, closed Sun

Post Office Bridge Street

Shopping Bridge Street; Wood Street; High Street; Henley Street (Early closing Thur)

Market Day Fri (Rother Street)

Theatres Royal Shakespeare Theatre, Waterside; The Other Place, Southern Lane. Box office for both theatres Tel (0789) 295623

Events Shakespeare Birthday Celebrations (nearest Sat to Apr 23); Boat Club Annual Regatta (3rd Sat in Jun); Stratford-upon-Avon Festival (last 2 weeks in Jul); Mop Fair (Oct 12)

Tours Guide Friday, 13 Waterside, offer bus tours of the town including Anne Hathaway's Cottage and Mary Arden's House, starting from Clopton Bridge. There are 5 tours daily in the summer and 2 tours daily in the winter. Inquiries: Tel (0789) 294466

Anyone who is in Stratford-upon-Avon on the Saturday nearest the 23rd April will quickly appreciate the town's significance: it is the day set aside for the official birthday celebration of its most famous son, William Shakespeare. The very diversity of the assembled crowd proclaims the poet and playwright's world renown: Africans, Americans, Asians and Europeans mingle with the citizens of Stratford, united by a single interest – Shakespeare. Many have sprigs of rosemary in their buttonholes:

> There's rosemary, that's for remembrance; pray, love, remember: and there is pansies, that's for thoughts.

The lines, lamenting her father's death and Hamlet's madness, are Ophelia's, but the sprigs are a tribute to their 'onlie begetter', whose death fell on the same date as his birth, over 350 years ago. Through the town, in procession, the crowd moves from Bridge Street, past the half-timbered cottage in Henley Street, where the poet was born, to the riverside church where, in the chancel, lie the graves of Shakespeare and his family.

What sort of place was this town that was to spring into fame with the publication of Shakespeare's first folio in 1623?

The name, Stratford, means 'Street-ford' – a place where a street or road fords a river – and, in Roman times, a bridge (carrying the Roman road from Droitwich and Alcester to Banbury) crossed the Avon near the present Clopton Bridge. But archaeologists have found evidence of an earlier Celtic settlement on the present site of the town.

The Domesday Book refers to Stradforde, then part of the manor

Shakespeare Memorial

of the Bishop of Worcester who owned a mill there, bringing him an annual income of ten shillings, or 1000 eels.

John Leland, one of the earliest British antiquaries, described the town, which he must have visited some time between 1534 and 1543. It had, he wrote, 'two or three very lardge streets, besyde bake lanes. The town is reasonably well buyldyd of tymbar...' Leland was particularly impressed with the bridge built by one of the town's most generous benefactors, Sir Hugh Clopton, the Lord Mayor of London in 1491, who spent much of his life in Stratford. 'He made also the great and sumptuous bridge upon Avon at the este end of the town', Leland noted, 'Before there was but a poore bridge of tymbar, and no causey to come to it, whereby many poore folkys refused to cum to Stratford when Avon was up, or cominge thither stoode in jeoperdy of lyfe'.

As well as the bridge, Clopton added a new and splendid nave to the Guild Chapel, and, almost next door to the chapel, built his own house, New Place. This house was later bought by Shakespeare, after he had become rich and successful. Unfortunately, a later owner – an eccentric clergyman called Francis Gastrell – demolished the house in 1759, following a dispute with the town council. The town was so incensed that an order was made that no one of that name was ever again to reside at Stratford.

Until 1547, when the Chantries Act dispersed all religious foundations, the town was ruled by the Guild of the Holy Cross, an Augustinian fraternity of men and women. The Guild provided and maintained what social amenities the town then had: a grammar school for the children, almshouses for the old and infirm, and religious services in their own Guild Chapel. There was also a college of priests to serve what is now the parish church – hence its name, the Collegiate Church of the Holy Trinity.

But if, three and a half centuries ago, Stratford-upon-Avon was no more than a small market town, the 23rd April, 1564 – the day on which William Shakespeare was born – was to alter its subsequent history and development, and to transform it, for the world at large, into Shakespeare's town. And today, its main activity is to provide for the needs of the 350,000 tourists who come to the town each year to visit the house where he was born, the places where his family lived and the theatre which, season after season, produces some of the best performances of his masterpieces.

Places of Interest
*Descriptions of these places are given in
the Walk, which follows. See Index for
page references. Admission fees apply to
all historic buildings. Those with an
* asterisk are administered by the
Shakespeare Birthday Trust, and a
reduced inclusive ticket is available to
these five properties*

Historic Buildings

* **Shakespeare's Birthplace** and
Shakespeare Centre Henley Street
Apr-Oct 9-7 (closing 6pm Sep, 5pm
Oct); Nov-Mar 9-4.30

* **Hall's Croft** Old Town
Apr-Oct 9-6, Sun 2-6; Nov-Mar
9-12.45 & 2-4, closed Sun

* **New Place** Chapel Lane
Hours as Hall's Croft

Nash's House Chapel Street
Hours as Hall's Croft

Harvard House High Street
Apr-Oct 9-1 & 2-6, Sun 2-6; Nov-Mar,
Thur, Fri & Sat 10-1 & 2-4

* **Anne Hathaway's Cottage** Shottery
Hours as Shakespeare's Birthplace

* **Mary Arden's House** Wilmcote
Hours as Hall's Croft

Churches

Holy Trinity (Shakespeare's Tomb)
Summer 8.30-7, Sun 2-5; winter
8.30-4, Sun 2-5

Guild Chapel Chapel Lane

Museums and Galleries

Arms and Armour Museum
Sheep Street
Daily 10-6

Motor Museum Shakespeare Street
An exhibition of vintage cars in a
'20s setting.
Apr-Oct 9.30-6; Nov-Mar 10-4

'The World of Shakespeare'
Waterside
25 life-size tableaux combined with
music and light and sound effects bring
Shakespearian England to life.
Daily 10-5.30

Clopton Bridge

Hotels & Historic Inns

(THF) A Trusthouse Forte Hotel

The Falcon
Chapel Street, Stratford-upon-Avon
CV37 6HA
Tel (0789) 5777
Shakespeare would have known *The
Falcon* as a private house, for it did
not become an inn until 1640. It is a
half-timbered building with lattice
windows, and contains panelling from
Shakespeare's last home, New Place,
demolished in 1759. The Shakespeare
Club was founded here in 1824.

The Shakespeare (THF)
Chapel Street, Stratford-upon-Avon
CV37 6ER
Tel (0789) 294771
Part of the inn may have been Sir Hugh
Clopton's Great House, built before

The Alveston Manor Hotel (THF)
Clopton Bridge, Stratford-upon-Avon
CV37 7HP
Tel (0789) 204581
This fine Tudor-style hotel near the River Avon is a conversion of a 16th-c. manor house. The building, formerly a religious house of the parish of Alveston (incorporated in the borough of Stratford in 1924) has a history of almost 1000 years. The bar has the original oak panelling from the hall of the manor, and many of the bedrooms have the original oak beams. The beautiful 7-acre garden is famous as the scene of the first production of Shakespeare's *Midsummer's Night Dream*.

The Swan's Nest Hotel (THF)
Bridgefoot, Stratford-upon-Avon
CV37 7LT
Tel (0789) 66761
On the bank of the Avon opposite the Royal Shakespeare Theatre and the town centre, this pleasant, traditional hotel is perfectly situated for visitors to Stratford. The *River Bar* is a popular venue, and the *Bewick Restaurant* is decorated with examples of the work of the wood-engraver Thomas Bewick (1753-1828).

Shakespeare's day, and the other part was known as 'the Five Gables'. Together they have nine gables. This famous half-timbered building probably did not become an inn until the 18th c., when it was popular with actors.

The White Swan (THF)
Rother Street, Stratford-upon-Avon
CV37 6NH
Tel (0789) 297022
Possibly started as the house of a Stratford merchant *c.* 1450, this has been an inn since Shakespeare's time. With its black timbers, fine panelling and carved Jacobean mantelpiece, it was an American Red Cross centre in World War II. The original living room has 16th-c. paintings of scenes from the Apocrypha preserved on its walls.

Walking tour Ideally the visitor to Stratford should start his tour at the home of Shakespeare's mother, Mary Arden, in Wilmcote, and then trace the poet's life through the houses that are associated with him. Unfortunately, two of the most interesting houses are some way out of the town: Mary Arden's House at Shottery. It is therefore suggested that the itinerary should concentrate first on those houses that are in town. Then either by car or by public transport, Shottery and Wilmcote should be visited.

Shakespeare's Birthplace Shakespeare's father, John, was a glove maker and wool dealer. He owned the two cottages in Henley Street, which have now been converted to form one house. As

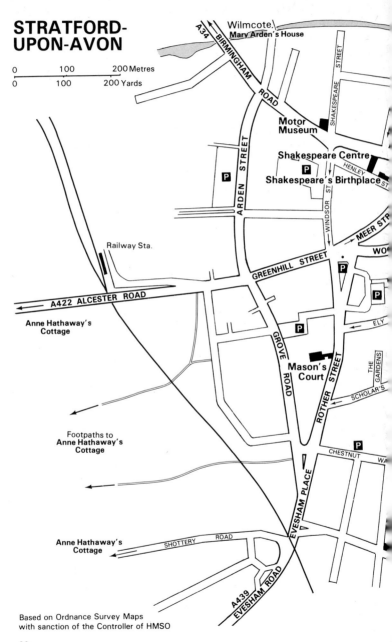

STRATFORD-UPON-AVON

Wilmcote,
Mary Arden's House

A34

BIRMINGHAM ROAD

SHAKESPEARE STREET

Motor Museum

Shakespeare Centre

Shakespeare's Birthplace

HENLEY ST

ARDEN STREET

WINDSOR ST

MEER STR

WO

Railway Sta.

GREENHILL STREET

A422 ALCESTER ROAD

Anne Hathaway's Cottage

GROVE ROAD

ELY

Mason's Court

ROTHER STREET

THE GARDENS

SCHOLAR'S

Footpaths to
Anne Hathaway's Cottage

CHESTNUT WA

EVESHAM PLACE

Anne Hathaway's Cottage

SHOTTERY ROAD

A439 EVESHAM ROAD

0   100   200 Metres
0   100   200 Yards

Based on Ordnance Survey Maps
with sanction of the Controller of HMSO

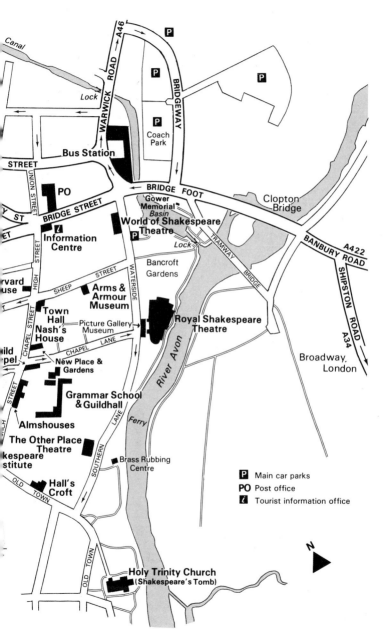

27

seen from the road, John Shakespeare's home was the left-hand cottage, and the one on the right the shop from which he ran his business. In 1557 he married Mary Arden, one of eight daughters who grew up in the farm house at Wilmcote. The Birthplace is now entered through the new **Shakespeare Centre**, a modern building designed by Laurence Williams and completed in 1964. The Centre houses the combined libraries of the Shakespeare Birthplace Trust and the Royal Shakespeare Theatre. It also has all the facilities of a modern study centre. From the Centre a path leads into the pretty, well-kept garden that surrounds John Shakespeare's cottage. Inevitably the Birthplace has been considerably restored: it was bought for the nation in 1847, for the then quite excessive price of £3000, a reflection of the extreme historic importance of the building. Originally the cottages formed part of a complete terrace, but the houses on either side were demolished to reduce the risk of fire.

The ground floor of the Birthplace would have been the main living room and kitchen, and now has furniture of the 16th and 17th c. Upstairs is reached by a narrow staircase: here the rooms show less evidence of restoration. The uneven elm boards are worn by the feet of countless visitors, and the low ceilings have their original trusses and tie beams. New lattice windows look out over the garden to the streets of modern Stratford. The room immediately above the living room is the actual room where, according to a well-authenticated tradition, Shakespeare was born.

From the Birthplace, walk down Henley Street into Bridge Street, certainly one of the 'very lardge streets' referred to by John Leland. Now, few houses of Shakespeare's period remain. It is a short street and the River Avon and the Clopton Bridge are soon in sight; to the right are the *Bancroft Gardens* which surround the Royal Shakespeare Theatre. Do not digress into the gardens before looking at the famous *Shakespeare Memorial*, a bronze statue on a high pedestal, with four separate

Hall's Croft

corner statues of Lady Macbeth, Prince Hal, Hamlet and Falstaff; this was designed by Lord Ronald Gower in 1880. A little further on is the old *Tramway Bridge*, now a footbridge of great charm, from where it is possible to get a good view of the 15th-c. **Clopton Bridge**, with its 14 arches of mellowed grey stone spanning the Avon.

It is now pleasant to wander along the banks of the Avon, dominated here by the **Royal Shakespeare Theatre**. This building replaced the original Shakespeare Memorial Theatre of 1879, built by the brewer Charles Flower, which burnt down in 1926 (part of the old building, now a picture gallery and museum, survives on the W side). The present building, designed by Elizabeth Scott, was completed in 1932.

Further on, the river bank walk leads past the old music room which now serves as a *Brass Rubbing Centre*. Ahead is the graceful spire of **Holy Trinity Church**, where Shakespeare and his children were baptised, and where he himself was buried.

The church is approached from the N by a stately avenue of trees. The twelve on the left are said to represent the twelve tribes of Israel, the eleven on the right the eleven faithful apostles; the one standing slightly back is for Mathias, who took the place of the treacherous Judas.

A church has stood on this site since Saxon times. The present building is partly 13th-14th-c. (transepts, N and S aisles, tower and nave piers) and partly Perpendicular of the late 15th- early 16th c. (chancel, clerestory, W window and porch). The spire is 18th-c.

The visitor wishing to see Shakespeare's Monument will proceed to the E end. At the top of the N aisle is the *Clopton Chapel*, containing tombs and memorials of the Clopton family. Most important are: (S side) cenotaph of Stratford's great benefactor, Sir Hugh Clopton (d. 1496) who became Lord Mayor of London and is buried in the capital; (E side) marble Renaissance monument with effigies of Joyce Clopton (d. 1635) and her husband George Carew, Earl of Totnes and Master in Ordnance to James I; and (N side) altar tomb with effigies of William Clopton (d. 1592) and his wife, with their seven children in a sculptured frieze above.

To the left of the crossing, the N transept, now the Vestry, is closed by a late 15th-c. screen. Passing through the choir screen (early 16th-c.) the *chancel* is entered. The choir stalls have fine 15th-c. misericords: wood carvings depicting medieval domestic scenes, birds, flowers and animals. The chancel also contains (to the W of the altar rail) the broken 15th-c. font in which Shakespeare was probably baptised, the Chained Bible (1611) used during Shakespeare's lifetime and photos of the pages of the parish register recording Shakespeare's baptism and burial. The entry of his baptism (1564) reads: 'April 26, Gulielmus filius Johannes Shakspere'; that of his burial (1616): 'April 26, Will Shakespeare Gent.'

E of the altar rail is *Shakespeare's grave* marked by a stone with the inscription:

> Good frend for Jesus sake forbeare,
> To digg the dust enclosed here.
> Blese be ye man yt spares thes stones,
> And curst be he yt moves my bones.

Beside Shakespeare's grave are those of his wife Anne, his daughter Susannah and other members of the family. The *monument*, on the N wall of the chancel,

was erected in 1623. It is the work of Gerard Janssen, and enshrines a bust of Shakespeare which was presumably authenticated as a true likeness by his family. It has now become the portrait that is most generally associated with Shakespeare and from which the frontispiece of the folios must have been taken.

Leaving the church by the N door and going straight ahead along Old Town, **Hall's Croft** is on the right. This house belonged to John Hall, a doctor who married Shakespeare's daughter in 1607. The Halls lived in this house until Shakespeare's death in 1616, when they moved to his house in New Place. Hall's Croft was bought by the Shakespeare Birthplace Trust in 1949 and was restored as nearly as possible to its original state. It is a timber-framed house of the late 16th c. and it is now furnished in the style of a middle-class Tudor home. It also contains a fascinating collection of medical items of this period, and records of cases that were treated by Dr Hall; the garden that surrounds the house is completely enclosed by walls, and is the most 'Shakespearean' of the Stratford gardens. Much of it was replanted when the building was restored in 1950.

Leaving Hall's Croft turn right into Church Street. On the left is **Mason's Croft**, an 18th-c. house that once belonged to Marie Corelli, who settled in Stratford and became something of a local character, striving to rule the town – and particularly the Shakespeare monuments – in a way that the townspeople found too overbearing to be acceptable. She was, however, instrumental in preserving many important buildings (see Harvard House). Mason's Croft is now the Shakespeare Institute of the University of Birmingham.

On the opposite side of the street, behind a row of almshouses, built *c.* 1427, but since enlarged and altered, is the **Grammar School** (not open to the public), where as a small boy, Shakespeare probably learnt 'small Latin and less Greek'. His desk – or what is believed to have been his desk – has been re-moved to the Birthplace, but the spot where it is reputed to have stood is marked with a small notice: 'Near this spot according to an old tradition handed down from scholar to scholar and attested by one whose schooldays fell in the early years of the XIX cen-tury, sat as a schoolboy William Shakes-peare'. On the corner of Church Street and Chapel Lane is the **Guild Chapel**, or the Chapel of the Guild of the Holy Cross, which was founded some time before 1269. It was enlarged in the late 15th c. by Sir Hugh Clopton, who built a new nave with large Perpendicular windows. The west tower is also late 15th-c. Over the chancel arch is a Doom wall painting, showing a Christ in Majesty with the Virgin and St John at the top.

Opposite the Guild Chapel is the site of **New Place**, the house which Shakes-peare bought in 1597 for £60 and where he died. Now, only the foundations can

Anne Hathaway's Cottage

be seen, but it is adjoined by the Elizabethan Knott Garden, a replica of a favourite type of Elizabethan garden: the garden is divided into four 'knotts' or beds, and each bed is made up of an intricate pattern of herbs and flowers. Beyond the Knott Garden is the Great Garden, which was originally the or-chard and kitchen garden of New Place.

Nash's House, which also adjoins the garden of New Place, can next be visited. This house once belonged to Thomas Nash, the first husband of Shakespeare's grand-daughter, Eliz-abeth Hall. Like the other houses it is furnished with Elizabethan furniture; it also contains a collection of local histori-cal and archaeological material.

Another building in the High Street (a continuation of Church Street) which is of particular interest is **Harvard House**, a highly ornate timber-framed house built in 1596 by Thomas Rogers, a butcher and alderman. His daughter, Katherine, was the mother of John Har-

vard, one of the founders of Harvard University in the United States. It was through the mediation of Marie Corelli that the house was bought for the University; it is now owned by the Harvard Memorial Trust. Inside the house there is a 17th-c. staircase, and upstairs a room with original pilastered panelling, and some early, though fairly crude, plasterwork.

Before leaving the town it is worth looking at the **Town Hall** in Sheep Street. It was built by Robert Newman in 1768 and the following year dedicated to the memory of Shakespeare by the famous actor David Garrick. In a niche on the N wall is a statue of the poet which was presented to the town by Garrick. In the council chamber there are some interesting portraits of Stratford personalities. Halfway along Sheep Street is the *Arms and Armour Museum*, with exhibits from the 15th-c. to the beginning of the First World War.

From Stratford the tour of houses with Shakespearian associations can be extended to Wilmcote, where the playwright's mother, Mary Arden, grew up, and Shottery, where he met his wife, Anne Hathaway. Shottery is a short and pleasant walk from Stratford, but Wilmcote is 3m NW off the A34. (In addition to the tour buses, there are ordinary bus and train services to Wilmcote).

Anne Hathaway's Cottage is perhaps the most famous of the Shakespeare houses. The 'cottage' was in fact a farmhouse, originally known as *Hewlands*, the farm of the Hathaways, yeoman farmers long established in the area. The lower part of the house is 15th-c. or even earlier, and the W half about 1600. The main living room was formerly an open 'hall'; it has original panelling and an inglenook fireplace. In the kitchen the bake-oven is still intact. Upstairs there are the bedrooms, the largest containing the famous Hathaway bed, a finely carved Elizabethan four-poster. Most of the furniture in the cottage belonged to the Hathaway family.

The garden and orchards around the cottage form much of its attraction, and make a perfect setting for its romantic story: it was in these surroundings that Shakespeare, at the age of eighteen, courted a bride seven years older than he.

Mary Arden's House is a pleasant farmhouse. Until 1930, when it was acquired by the Shakespeare Birthplace Trust, it was still used as a farmhouse; as a result it has been little modernised, and is still almost in its original state. Most of the building is early 16th-c.; the walls are half-timbered on a stone foundation. The timber came from the Forest of Arden and the stone was quarried in Wilmcote itself. The farm buildings – the big stone barns and a dovecote – are now used to house a good collection of farm carts and implements. After the bustle of busy Stratford, the visitor will appreciate the peace and tranquillity of this lovely house.

First you enter the kitchen, with its massive open fireplace, where all the meals of the house would have been prepared; there is a good collection of early cooking implements but, originally, there would have been a bread oven to the right of the fireplace. The kitchen has an early paved stone floor.

The living room with its great refectory table was the room where the family met, ate and received their guests. Formerly, this would have been open to the roof, but at a later date it was converted into a two-storey building by the insertion of a first floor, supported by massive beams. There are benches on either side of the table, and at the head an uncomfortable-looking wooden arm chair used exclusively by the head of the family. Mary Arden, the future wife of John Shakespeare, was the youngest of eight daughters. Before her marriage she would have slept on the floor of the living room or the kitchen with the other unmarried members of the household and the servants – thus when a woman was 'bedded', she would literally have slept in a bed for the first time in her life.

Gazetteer

excluding Stratford-upon-Avon (p.22)

This includes information on the location, history and main features of the places of interest in the region. Visiting hours for all places open to the public are shown in 'The Best of the Region'. Asterisks indicate references to other Gazetteer entries

We have taken as our practical western border the Cotswold Edge, to the east of the M5, the Warwickshire and Oxfordshire borders to the north and east and the Gloucestershire border to the south. Beyond these borders, but very much a part of the Cotswolds, are the small towns of Broadway, Chipping Norton and Burford, with their local villages. Near Stratford-upon-Avon the great houses of Compton Wynyates, Charlecote Park, Honington Hall and Upton are included.

The Swan, Bibury

EC: Early closing   MD: Market Day
Populations over 10,000 shown
Map references after place names refer to map inside back cover
All places are in Gloucestershire unless shown otherwise

Adlestrop D2
Village off A436, 4m E of Stow-on-the-Wold

This village was brought to fame by Edward Thomas (d. 1917), in his poem which begins:

Yes, I remember Adlestrop
The name – because one afternoon
Of heat the express-train drew up there
Unwontedly. It was late June.

No one left and no one came.
On the bare platform. What I saw
Was Adlestrop – only the name. . .

The railway has since been closed, and the station sign which Edward Thomas saw is now in the bus shelter, with his poem engraved on a plaque on the seat below. Jane Austen used to visit her uncle, Theophilus Leigh, at the Rectory. The *Church of St Mary Magdalene* was rebuilt in 1765, almost certainly by Sanderson Miller, who in 1762 rebuilt nearby *Adlestrop Park* in 'Gothick' style: Humphrey Repton was the landscape gardener. This property has been in the hands of the Leigh family since the mid-17th c.

Aldsworth C3
Village on A433 between Burford and Bibury

Aldsworth is set just far enough back from the road not to be spoiled by it. It has a distinct early 19th-c. air, because the houses were built for grooms and jockeys during the heyday of the nearby Bibury Racecourse – the 1833 Derby winner was trained locally.

St Bartholomew's Church lies a little to the W of the village. It dates from 1151 but was heavily restored in 1877, although there is a well preserved N aisle dating from around 1500. The exterior has fine gargoyles, particularly on the N side.

Ampney Crucis, Ampney St Peter, Ampney St Mary, Down Ampney C4
Villages near Cirencester, the first three respectively 2½, 3½ and 4½m to the E (A417), Down Ampney 5m SE off A419

Ampney (pronounced Amney) **Crucis** is a straggling, not particularly attractive village, but the area immediately N of the main road is full of interest. The Ampney Brook flows under a bridge and past *Upper Mill*, which has an 1804 datestone but is now a house. Down a little lane is the *Holy Rood Church*, Saxon in origin, with a fine Norman chancel arch and traces of medieval wall paintings. Of particular interest is the 16th-c. tomb with lifesize effigies of George Lloyd and his wife and the figures of their five sons and seven daughters on the tomb-chest. In the churchyard is a fine 15th-c. cross; the gabled head, found walled up in the church, was restored *c*. 1860. The name of the village is related not to the cross but to the church: the village is referred to in the Domesday Book as 'Omenie Holy Rood'. *Ampney Park*, a Tudor manor house with a Georgian wing and 19th-c. additions, is just W of the church.

Just S of the A417 between Ampney Crucis and Ampney St Peter is the Norman *Church of Ampney St Mary*. Though still used, it is now completely isolated from the village of **Ampney St Mary**, 1m to the NE. This was formerly the village of Ashbrook; the old Ampney St Mary was possibly abandoned because of the Black Death. Despite the buttresses, the walls of the little church are visibly bulging. The carved tympanum over the blocked N doorway is thought to represent the Lion of Righteousness triumphing over the agents of evil, aided by a griffin. Inside, the church is pleasantly light, which makes it easier to see the fragments of medieval wall paintings that would once have covered the entire church.

Further down the road is **Ampney St Peter**, a little stone village set just off the main road. *St Peter's Church*, which was largely rebuilt by Sir George Gilbert Scott in 1878, is rather dull. ½m to the SE is *Ranbury Ring*, an Iron Age hill fort.

Down Ampney is the birthplace of Ralph Vaughan Williams, the composer (1872-1958), and is immortalized in his hymn of the same name. The church, *All Saints*, and the manor house are situated away from the village, amidst lush meadows. The church was consecrated *c*. 1265; the tower is Early English with a 14th-c. spire, the porch

is 15th-c. Inside, the wealth of richly carved late 19th-c. woodwork is slightly overwhelming, but there is a fine 17th-c. monument of two praying knights in the N transept. Note also the 14th-c. tomb with recumbent effigies in the S transept, the 13th-c. red-painted flowers on the arcade arches, and, as a curiosity, the massive ladder under the tower. Neighbouring *Down Ampney House* is 15th-c. with an open hall lit by two large mullioned and transomed windows with buttresses either side.

Asthall   D3
Oxfordshire. Village off A40, 2½m E of Burford

A delightful village, with the River Windrush flowing placidly through the water meadows. The gabled early 17th-c. *Manor House* was once the home of Speaker Lenthall of the Long Parliament. More recently it was the childhood home of the Mitford sisters before the family moved to *Swinbrook*. *St Nicholas' Church* is late Norman with Transitional arches in the nave arcade resting on squat round pillars. Interesting architectural details are the bird beak corbels in the N aisle: an image repeated round the chancel arch. The N transept has a stone effigy of Lady Joan Cornwall, who owned the manor in the middle of the 14th c., also 14th-c. stained glass. The chancel has Victorian wall paintings.

The Maytime Inn is a good place for lunch (open Sundays): children are welcome. (See also *Walk 1*, p.18.)

Aston Blank (Cold Aston)   C3
Village off A429, 3½m W of Bourton-on-the-Water

Originally plain Aston, it became Cold Aston in 1255 and Aston Blank in 1535. This high wold village has a Norman church, *St Andrew's*, with a good Baroque wall monument to Giles Carter (died 1664); the nave and chancel are Norman, the W tower Perpendicular. There is a little green in the village, with a large sycamore tree and a pub that probably dates back to the 17th c. It is worth coming here just for the views – wonderful all round this area.

Stratford-upon-Avon   Left: Shakespeare's Birthplace
Above: Shakespeare's Memorial, Holy Trinity Church

Avening B4
Village on B4014, 2½m SE of Nailsworth

The rambling village of Avening is built along the banks of the River Avon, which is crossed by an attractive bridge at the centre of the village. The large cruciform *Holy Cross Church* is said to have been founded by Queen Matilda. It has a rare stone vaulted chancel, and a fine Norman N doorway; the timber roof of the nave dates from the 14th c. In the N transept is a kneeling effigy of Henry Brydges, once a notorious pirate: behind the organ is a good collection of rustic Baroque stone tablets. *Avening Court*, the old manor house where Henry Brydges finally settled down to lead a blameless life, *c.*1600, has been so much altered that little of the original building remains; the Elizabethan-style façade dates back only to the late 19th c.

Between Avening and Nailsworth is *Longford's Mill*, famous for making red cloth for Army ceremonial uniform. It is beautifully situated by the edge of a lake in a thickly wooded valley. There are also several long barrows and tumuli to the N of Avening, a large pillar of stone called the *Tingle Stone*, and *Norn's Tump*, thought to be 5000 years old.

Bagendon B3/C3
Village off A435, 4m N of Cirencester

It is curious to learn that this little village, with its small church and handful of cottages, was in prehistoric times the capital of the important Dobunni tribe, and virtually the mother town of Roman Cirencester – Corinium Dobunnorum. **Bagendon Dykes** (½m E and SE of the village) are a system of Iron Age ditches which with a wooded scarp served to enclose the Dobunni capital. Finds from the site are in the Corinium Museum, Cirencester.

St Margaret's Church is probably Saxon, certainly early Norman. As this church has always been liable to flood, the chancel was raised above the nave in medieval times. In 1832 the nave was also raised by 2ft, but this proved ineffective and the former level of the nave was restored.

Barnsley C3
Village on A433, 4m NE of Cirencester

An exceptionally pretty village, with mostly 17th to early 19th-c. cottages, spoilt only by its position on a busy main road. The attractive Norman *St Mary's Church*, with its unusual tower (the gabled top was added in the early 17th c.) was restored in 1847 but retains details of the original building.

Barnsley House, in the village, was built in 1697, and altered *c.* 1840. The *Garden* was first laid out in 1770, and contains an 18th-c. Gothic summerhouse and neo-classical temple, but in its present form is very much the personal creation of Rosemary and David Verey.

Reached by a footpath N of the village is *Barnsley Park*, an early Georgian Baroque mansion. Built 1720-31 from locally quarried pale golden limestone, it is a fine house (not open to the public). John Nash decorated the Library, which housed Isaac Newton's books for over 100 years. Nash also designed the Orangery and the little octagonal park building known as *Bibury Lodge* or *The Pepper Pot*. A Roman villa is being excavated in the grounds.

Barringtons, Great and Little D3
Villages off A40, 3½m W of Burford

The best thing about **Great Barrington** is its large, light church, **St Mary's**. It retains the original Norman chancel arch, but the unusual square-headed windows, clerestory, and flat, panelled nave roof, with its carved bosses and stone corbels, date from *c.*1511. The chancel contains several monuments to the Talbot family, who bought Barrington Park from the Brays in 1734, including one to Mary, Countess Talbot (died 1787) by Joseph Nollekens. The finest monument, just inside the door, is to the Bray children. The two children, here shown being conducted over the clouds of heaven by a winged angel, died of smallpox in 1720, aged eight and eleven. This monument to them remains moving to this day.

Just next to the church is *Barrington Park*. The 16th-c. manor house was burnt down a year after the Talbots bought it, and the present Palladian mansion was built 1736-8, possibly by William Kent. One can get some impression of the beautifully landscaped park from the road – especially through the lovely wrought-iron gates on the way to the Rissingtons – but the house itself cannot be visited. The village has a rather neglected air, as several of the houses are semi-derelict – apparently because the owner refuses to sell.

The two Barringtons are separated by the River Windrush. The road between them, passing *The Fox Inn* by the bridge, runs just above the meadows and willows of the river valley.

Little Barrington is a delightful village, built round a hummocky, bowl-like village green, with a brook running across it. Goats and ducks add to its charm. *St Peter's Church* is a little to the E of the village, overlooking the river valley and Great Barrington beyond. It has an uneven flagged floor and some good Norman stonework, particularly the doorway and the round arches of the nave arcade. The carved tympanum set in the N outside wall shows Christ in Majesty with angels.

Batsford   C2
Village off A429, 2m NW of Moreton-in-Marsh
Batsford, the mansion, village and park, is almost entirely the creation of one man, Algernon Bertram Freeman-Mitford, later Lord Redesdale. He was British Ambassador in Tokyo in 1850 and during his time there acquired a great deal of knowledge about the creation of wild treed gardens. The **Batsford Park Arboretum** is now one of the most interesting collections of trees and bamboos in the country.

Lord Redesdale was the grandfather of the Mitford sisters (The family moved to **Asthall* in the '20s). At Batsford his creative activity was not limited to landscaping his garden: he also demolished the Georgian family house and built the present one (1888-92) in traditional Cotswold style. The architects were Sir Ernest George and Peto. Even the village was entirely re-modelled to match his mansion. The *Church* was rebuilt in 1861-2 in neo-Norman style. Inside, an over-ornate screen running along the W wall protects the family pew, described by Goodhart Rendel as 'the Holy Hon's cupboard'.

Baunton   C3
Village on A435, 1½m N of Cirencester
The village itself is rather straggling, with some sadly derelict barns, but the *Church of St Mary Magdalene* is well worth looking at. Inside, it is dominated by the exceptionally well preserved, life-sized 14th-c. wall painting of St Christopher, shown carrying the Child through a stream full of fishes. The church also contains a complete embroidered 15th-c. altar frontal.

The 16th/17th-c. *Manor Farmhouse* has some fine large barns.

Belas Knap   B2
Ancient site off A46, 2m S of Winchcombe
The easiest way to reach Belas Knap is to leave Winchcombe on the A46, going towards Cheltenham, then to take the first left turn past the church, and to follow the signs for Belas Knap and Brockhampton. The beginning of the footpath, which goes off to the right, is well signposted, as is the whole ¾m route. It is a marvellous walk, with fine views of Winchcombe and Sudeley Castle.

About 4000 years old, the 180ft-long barrow was a Stone Age burial mound. Of about 50 barrows in the Cotswolds, this is the finest of the 'false entrance' type. There are three small chambers with entrances from outside, which can be crawled through, and a massive false doorway between two horns at the N end. This may have been to outwit tomb robbers, or possibly to confuse the evil spirits as to the true position of the dead. It is built of huge limestone slabs, and surrounded by a drystone wall like those being built today. When it was opened in 1863-5, 38 skeletons were found, and some Roman remains. The barrow was restored in 1930-31.

From Belas Knap it is possible to walk across high ground 2m W to **Cleeve Common*.

Beverston B4
Village on A4135, 2m W of Tetbury

Built by the Beverley family in the 13th-14th c., **Beverston Castle** is one of the Cotswold's few surviving medieval castles. It is approached by the narrow path to the church, and the visitor's first sight is of its massive, semi-ruined walls towering over dank woods. Here, it seems, is the true Gothic ruin. Then a gateway by a ruined tower offers a glimpse of the courtyard of the rebuilt wing of the castle, now a private house of great attraction. This wing was added after 1597, when the Berkeleys sold the castle. Twice besieged, the castle was taken by the Parliamentarians in 1644. (Open by appointment only.)

Originally Norman, **St Mary's Church** was rebuilt by various owners of the castle in the 13th-15th c. The Norman tower, topped by a 15th-c. belfry, has a Saxon sculpture of the Resurrection set into it. There is a fine Norman S doorway leading into the S aisle. Here, the 13th-c. S arcade of three pointed arches has Norman columns with stiff-leaf capitals. The chancel and Berkeley Chapel, connected by a squint passage, were built by Thomas Lord Berkeley in 1361. The church was restored in 1844 by Lewis Vulliamy, who designed the nave roof with its ingenious trusses. He also designed many of the cottages in the village.

Bibury C3
Village on A433, 7m NE of Cirencester, 10m SW of Burford

William Morris was one of the first of the many admirers of this village, undoubtedly one of the most beautiful in England. The River Coln meandering along the roadside, and the famous Arlington Row of Cotswold cottages relate perfectly to their setting. Inevitably the village attracts many tourists during the summer, but this should not discourage the visitor from appreciating its beauty and tranquillity. In the past, the village was famous for a different reason: Bibury was once the headquarters of the oldest racing club in the country. Charles II is said to have come to the

Arlington Row, Bibury

race meetings three times, and in 1681 the Newmarket spring meeting was transferred here.

The village straggles along 1m of the A433 on either side of the river: the best idea is to park near the stone bridge by *The Swan Hotel* (if there's space) and walk from the mill, on the other side of the river, to the church at the far end of the village.

Arlington Mill was built in the 17th c. on the site of an older mill mentioned in the Domesday Book; it was strengthened, and the buttresses added, in the 19th c. It was a working mill until 1914, but unfortunately the mill machinery has not survived. The machinery that can now be seen working (powered by electricity, not water) was brought from North Cerney. David Verey supervised the restoration of the mill in 1966 and set it up as a museum of local history (*Cotswold Country Museum*). Its main features are the collection of farm carts and machinery, and rooms designed to show how the local people lived and worked. It also has an excellent collection of furniture by the Cotswold craftsman Ernest Gimson, who worked in the early part of this century at Daneway House, Sapperton.

Next to the mill is *Bibury Trout Farm*, open to the public who can buy fish here. Opposite lies the water meadow known as *Rack Isle*, where the local weavers used to dry their cloth on racks: it is now a bird sanctuary. On the far side of the meadow stand the little cottages of **Arlington Row**, with their tall, steep-pitched roofs and irregular shapes. The weavers who lived here used to supply cloth for fulling at the mill. The cottages date back to *c.* 1380: they were probably built as a sheephouse, and converted into dwellings in the 17th c. They are now owned by the National Trust.

Recrossing the river, the road is followed to the E end of the village to **St Mary's Church**. This church dates back to Saxon times, and despite extensive rebuilding parts of the original church remain. The chancel arch rises from jambs topped by Saxon capitals,

and part of a carved Saxon gravestone is embedded in its outside N wall. Also Saxon is the circular window with a splayed opening in the S wall of the nave. The N nave arcade is late Norman: note particularly the massive circular pier. There is a 13th-c. font, and the N aisle has early 18th-c. brasses. A beautiful exterior feature is the late Norman N door.

Next to the church is *Bibury Court*, largely built by Sir Thomas Sackville and now an hotel, its grounds running down to the River Coln. There is an excellent view of the house on the way down from **Coln St Aldwyns*. Note the little round dovecote opposite the farm gates, with its conical roof and turret, and the delightful group of Cotswold cottages grouped round the church gates.

Birdlip   B3
Village on B4070, 5m S of Cheltenham

The village is built at the top of Birdlip Hill, a long, steep ascent to the Cotswold escarpment from the Gloucester Vale below. There was a staging post for horses at the top even in Roman times, for the present road follows the exact path of Ermine Street, the Roman road from Gloucester to Cirencester and beyond. This explains why there are no diagonals or hairpin bends to lessen the steepness of the 1:5 slope. Roman remains have been found all round *The Royal George Inn*, and one of the only two Iron Age mirrors ever to be discovered also comes from Birdlip. It and items of jewellery found here are thought to have belonged to a queen of the Dobunni tribe who ruled this region before the Romans.

Bishop's Cleeve   B2
Village on A435, 3m N of Cheltenham

Rapidly becoming a northern suburb of Cheltenham (with the famous racecourse in between), Bishop's Cleeve still has an *Old Rectory* that David Verey considers 'probably the oldest and most splendid parsonage in the county'. Now known as *Cleeve Hall* and used as offices, it stands at the approach to the village on the Cheltenham road. Built by the Bishop of Worcester *c.* 1250, it was altered by another bishop in 1667. All the windows of the house are 17th-c., and one of the rooms has its walls decorated with an 1810 mural painting. There is a possibly 16th-c. dovecote in the garden. An early 15th-c. *Tithe Barn*, now used as a hall and community centre, stands opposite the rectory. The village has several timber-framed cottages.

The parish **Church of St Michael and All Angels** is late Norman-Transitional, *c.*1170, with much rebuilding in the 14th c. The church tower was rebuilt in 1700. The church has a rare, two-tiered Norman porch and the W front has a fine Norman doorway. Inside, there are some wall paintings and fragments of 14th- and 15th-c. stained glass in the S aisle. Monuments include an unknown knight, *c.*1270-1320, in the S transept, a recumbent 14th-c. effigy of a lady in the S aisle and, in the same part, an alabaster monument with recumbent effigies on a tomb-chest to Richard Delabere (d. 1636) and his wife.

1m E of the village are Cleeve Hill and **Cleeve Common.*

Bisley B3
Village off A419 or B4070, 4m E of Stroud

Bisley is a large, compact hillside village, full of pleasant houses and cottages, its streets running at different levels and unexpected angles.

The large 13th-c. *All Saints' Church* was rather over-restored by Thomas Keble's curate in 1862 (Thomas Keble was John Keble's younger brother). However, there are several things worth looking at inside the church: an early 13th-c. effigy of a knight; the tablet to Thomas Keble and his son, also Thomas, in the chancel; a small 16th-c. brass on the wall of the S aisle; good stone corbels in the N aisle; a series of 11th- and 12th-c. decorated stone coffin lids set into the wall; and the Norman font with its extraordinary, primitively carved Victorian base. Outside in the churchyard is a 'poor soul's light', used

to hold candles during masses for the poor; it is thought to be the only one in England out of doors. Thomas Keble was also responsible for restoring the ancient springs below the church, known as *Bisley Wells* or *The Seven Springs*. Here on Ascension Day the ancient ceremony of well dressing takes place.

Next to the church is *Over Court*, a splendid medieval house altered in the early 17th c. Elizabeth I is said to have stayed here. At the top of George Street is the village *Lock-up* dated 1824, with two cells and heavily barred doors. Just beyond that, facing down the street, is *The Bear Inn*, which has unusual pillars supporting the first floor.

Bledington D2
Village on B4450, 4m SE of Stow-on-the-Wold

A pleasant village built round a large green with a stream crossed by several footbridges. **St Leonard's Church** is quite exceptional. It is, on a miniature scale, not unlike the great Cotswold wool churches, and like the wool churches it is a church of Norman origin greatly enlarged and improved in the 15th c. It was then that the tower was built, and the nave heightened to allow for a clerestory. An aisle was added on the S *c.*1200, but no aisle was ever built on the N: hence the magnificent double tier of windows in the N wall. The stonework in the church is all of the highest quality, as is the contemporary 15th-c. stained glass in the windows.

Blockley C2
Village on B4479, 4m NW of Moreton-in-Marsh

This large, attractive village has an interesting history. By 855 it had a minster church, and St Wulstan (1062-95) is supposed to have performed miracles here. The Bishops of Worcester bought the parish from King Burgred for 300 shillings in the 9th c. and it was only transferred from Worcestershire in 1931.

Blockley was once the hub of the local silk industry, and it seems likely that it was through the Rushout family, of nearby Northwick Park, that the industry was introduced to the village. The first Rushout to be connected with Blockley was a James Rushout born in 1644, the son of a wealthy Flemish immigrant (the fourth son of this line was to become the first Lord Northwick); the earliest mill to be used for throwing silk was leased in 1688. The silk mills seem to have flourished through the 18th c., and in 1824 there were eight mills working, employing, either in the mills or at home, more than 3000 people within a 10m radius of the village. The long High Street, running from the church up towards Dovedale Woods, is built alongside the stream that powered these mills. But by 1885 the Blockley silk industry was dead, and the mills were turned to other purposes – threshing, grinding corn, sawing wood, even piano-making.

The introduction of the silk trade was not the only benefit the Rushouts brought to Blockley. In 1868 the 3rd Lord Northwick restored the church; following an epidemic of cholera, he also built a complete sewerage system for the village, and installed a piped water supply from a reservoir at Dovedale. In 1884 Lord Northwick's son-in-law, Edward Spencer-Churchill, harnessed the water power to generate electricity, first for his own house and then for the village, making Blockley one of the first villages in the country to have electric light.

Northwick Park, 1m N of Blockley, was built from 1686 onwards; the E front was remodelled by Lord Burlington in 1732. It remained in the hands of the Rushout family until 1864, and is now a home for drug addicts.

The **Church of St Peter and St Paul** is large, with a Norman chancel and Gothic-style tower. There is a 1510 brass of a priest on the back of the sedilia, shown, uniquely, in full mass vestments, and another brass of a priest, wearing a cope, on the chancel floor. At the E end of the N aisle, which was added in the 14th c., is the Rushout family vault, containing some splendid tombs. Two busts on a monument of

c.1775 are signed by J.M. Rysbrack. Among the church's many other monuments is a splendid Baroque painted stone piece by Edward Woodward of Chipping Campden.

Beyond Dovedale is *Upton Wold*, an Anglo-Saxon village destroyed by the Black Death, now being excavated.

Bourton-on-the-Hill   C2
Village on A44, 2m W of Moreton-in-Marsh

The long village street, built on a steep hill, is dominated by *The Horse and Groom* inn at the top, with its graceful Georgian front. Even *St Lawrence's Church* is built on a terrace. Entered on the level through the 15th-c. N porch, its rear S porch opens onto the hillside. The Perpendicular church is Norman in origin, *c*. 1157.

The village was developed mainly in the 17th c., and there are two manor houses. Both *Manor Farmhouse*, at the top of the village, and *Bourton House*, at the bottom, were rebuilt in the 18th c. Bourton House is known for its great **Tithe Barn**, dated 1570. It is one of the largest in the Cotswolds, with seven bays, gabled porches, wide arched entrances and six buttresses.

The houses and gardens of *★Batsford* and *★Sezincote* are both 1m from the village (N and S turnings off the A44, E of the village).

Bourton-on-the-Water   C3
Small town on A429, 3m SW of Stow-on-the-Wold.
Event: Water Game (Late Summer Bank Hol Mon)

Sometimes ironically called 'the Venice of the Cotswolds' Bourton-on-the-Water, with its low stone footbridges spanning the clear waters of the Windrush, here flowing between broad grassy verges, does have a great many tourist attractions. This makes it fun for a family outing, but also makes it very overcrowded.

Best known are the Model Village and Birdland. The **Model Village** is an exact replica, scaled down to one ninth, of Bourton before the Second World War; it is built of locally quarried stone and includes a model of the model

village itself. **Birdland**, now world-famous, is the creation of Leonard Hill, who bought the 17th-c. manor house, *Chardawar*, in 1956. He restored the house and 3½-acre garden and began to collect birds from all over the world. He now has about 600 species, including many from the tropics. Bourton also has a *Butterfly Museum*, a *Motor Museum* housed in an 18th-c. water-mill, a *Model Railway* and the *Cotswold Perfumery*, where visitors can test the products. Another attraction is the *Windrush Trout Farm*, where visitors can view – and purchase – the fish. On the Late Summer Bank Holiday Monday there is the Water Game – five-a-side football played to FA rules in the River Windrush.

Bourton-on-the-Water must once have been a lovely little town, but it is now the most spoilt of any Cotswold town or village. Away from the main street, however, there is still much of historic interest. Of many attractive houses in the town, the Palladian-style *Harrington House*, completed *c.* 1740 and built of golden stone, is by far the most splendid.

St Lawrence's Church was completely rebuilt in the 19th c., but the 14th-c. chancel and the Georgian lead-domed tower were preserved, making it look most unlike a typical Cotswold church.

Just to the E of the village is *Salmonsbury*, an Iron Age hill fort. The site covers about 60 acres, and trial excavations have produced the foundations of circular huts, currency bars, pottery and tools.

See also *Walk 4*, p.19.

Brimpsfield B3
Village off A417, 6½m S of Cheltenham

The manor of Brimpsfield belonged to the Giffards until 1322, when John Giffard foolishly attacked Edward II's baggage train as the king was marching along nearby Ermine Street. Giffard was hanged and his castle demolished; all that can now be seen are the tree-covered moat and mounds of the foundations to the right of the churchyard (approaching the church). *St Michael's*

Church is reached by a footpath over a field. Originally Norman with a 15th-c. central tower, it was restored in 1884.

Brimscombe B4
Village off A419, 3m SE of Stroud

Brimscombe Port in the Golden Valley was once the headquarters of the Thames-Severn Canal Company and the trans-shipment point for goods carried up from the Severn. The valley is narrow, so the village is mainly built in terraces on the hillside. A few mills still stand, some in use, though no longer making cloth and no longer powered by water, and there are some good mill owners' houses just above the mills. The *Holy Trinity Church* was built in 1840.

1m to the N is *Nether Lypiatt Manor*, the home of Prince and Princess Michael of Kent. It is a charming square early 18th-c. house, of which Sacheverell Sitwell wrote: 'No house would compose so beautifully for a glass transparency'.

Broadway C2
Hereford and Worcester. Village on A44/A46, 15m NE of Cheltenham. EC Thur

Consisting mainly of a long, wide street, with broad grass verges and a green at one end and buildings of fine, mellow stone, Broadway is a very attractive village, not too much spoilt by the many tourists who come here. Indeed, the inns, teashops and antique shops can be a positive attraction to the traveller who has been driving round the countryside through tiny villages often without even a single shop.

The two oldest buildings in Broadway are *Abbot's Grange*, below the green and secluded behind yew hedges, and *Prior's Manse*, on the left going E up the main street. Both 14th-c., they are amongst the oldest houses in the county. But most of the houses in Broadway date from the 17th and 18th c., when the village was an important staging post: at one time there were 20 inns. One of the oldest is *The Lygon Arms*, built in 1620, when it was known as *The White Horse Inn*. Charles I and

Oliver Cromwell are said to have stayed here. The village declined with the coming of the railway, but it was 'discovered' towards the end of the 19th c. by William Morris and restored largely due to his influence.

A new church was built in 1840, leaving the 12th-c. *St Eadburgha's* – 1m S of the village on the way to Snowshill – untouched by the Victorians. Cruciform, with a central tower rising from four graceful arches, St Eadburgha's is set in meadows with a little stream at the bottom of the churchyard. Inside is an Elizabethan brass, a grand Baroque monument dated 1741, and a handsome marble monument to Sir Thomas Phillips (1792-1872), the book collector, who lived nearby as *Middle Hill House* and whose declared aim was 'to have one copy of every book in the world'.

To the E of the village the road ascends in a series of bends to *The Fish Inn*, 600ft above sea level, and to *Broadway Tower*, over 100ft up and the second highest point in the Cotswolds. The tower is said to have been built by the Earl of Coventry *c.* 1797 for his wife because she was so impressed by the fact that a bonfire lit there could be seen from the family seat at Croome Court, near Worcester. The tower was sold in 1827, and subsequent residents included Sir Thomas Phillips, who housed his antiquarian book collection here, and William Morris, who spent several holidays here with his friends Rossetti and Burne-Jones.

The site is famous for its views: on a clear day 12 counties can be seen. The tower is the centre of *Broadway Tower Country Park* and is used for exhibitions of local crafts, geology and natural history. The Country Park also has play and picnic areas, restaurants and nature walks.

Broadwell D2
Village off A429, 1½m NE of Stow-on-the-Wold

This attractive village is mainly built round a large green. *The Fox Inn* faces the green, and at the lower end the road runs through a ford. *St Paul's Church* stands well away from the village, in a

lovely setting. It is 12th-c. in origin, but was restored in the 1860s, when the Norman tympanum, carved with a Maltese Cross, was reset at the foot of the turret stairs. Inside the church, under a Renaissance canopy, are alabaster effigies of Herbert Weston (died 1635) and his wife and child, kneeling at a prayer desk. In the churchyard is a good collection of early 17th-c. table-tombs: one is carved with the figures of eight kneeling mourners. In the spring, the churchyard is full of daffodils and blue anemones.

Buckland C2
Village off A46, 2m SW of Broadway

A small, quiet village set below wooded hills at the edge of the Cotswold Scarp. The fine Early English **St Michael's Church** is full of interesting things, above all the E window, which has three panels of 15th-c. glass representing the Sacraments of Baptism and Confirmation (together), Holy Matrimony and Extreme Unction. William Morris was so impressed that he paid to have the window re-leaded, *c.* 1883. The other treasures of the church are an exquisitely embroidered 15th-c. blue velvet cope, a 16th-c. mazer bowl made of maplewood and silver, 15th-c. floor tiles, extensive 17th-c. seating and wainscoting, and a pre-Reformation painted roof. The gargoyles outside should not be missed.

The 16th-c. *Manor House* has been almost entirely rebuilt but, according to David Verey, **Buckland Rectory** is 'the oldest and most complete medieval parsonage house in the county still so used'. Its impressive 15th-c. *Great Hall* has an open timber roof and original stained glass in the NW windows.

Burford D3
Oxfordshire. Small town off A40, 22m E of Cheltenham. Event: Burford Dragon procession (Midsummer's Eve). EC Wed. Inf: Tel (099382) 2557

Known as the 'Gateway to the Cotswolds', Burford combines the two elements which have given the area its character and prosperity: wool and stone. The church and medieval merchants' houses stand as solid monu-

Gatehouse, Stanway

Left: Painswick Above: Lower Slaughter

ments both to the prosperous wool industry of the Middle Ages and the stone with which they were built (quarried from nearby Taynton, Stonesfield and other quarries in the area).

When the wool industry declined Burford still flourished as an important staging post. At the beginning of the 19th c., as many as 40 stage coaches passed through the town in one day. (The journey from Burford to London took 24 hours: the fare was 18s.) But in 1812 the road was rerouted to the S of the town – its present route – and the railway also bypassed Burford. The lost traffic spelt lost trade for the town and it was not to recover until the motor car and the tourists arrived in the 20th c.

The building and enlargement of the **Church of St John the Baptist** reflects the town's rise to prosperity. In 1175 it was a simple Norman building, a nave with a small tower. In the next 300 years there were various additions, including the transepts and a guild chapel (originally separate from the church, now incorporated as the Lady Chapel) and the heightening of the nave and tower. By 1475 the church was as we see it today, a complicated building with chapels and aisles at odd angles and on different levels. The enthusiasm of the merchants was too much for it, however, and with the additional weight of 700 tons of masonry and 30 tons of bells the tower seemed in danger of collapsing. To prevent this the Norman tower arches were filled in to give the building extra strength.

Inside the church, looking towards the crossing, the alterations to the height of the nave are shown by the different roof marks on the wall of the tower: within the tower itself, at the crossing, the blocked up Norman arches can be seen.

The tombs in Burford Church are of great interest. In the N aisle is that of *Edmund Harman* (d. 1577) and his wife Alice. The unusual wall monument has effigies of their children only, and is decorated with native figures – probably Brazilian Indians – though the reason for this is unknown. Harman was

barber-surgeon to Henry VIII, and in reward for his services was given Burford Priory for his lifetime.

In the N chapel is the elaborate canopied tomb of *Sir Lawrence Tanfield* (d. 1625) and Lady Tanfield, built by his widow without the permission of the authorities. Tanfield, a Burford man, was Lord Chief Baron of the Exchequer to James I. He bought the Priory *c.* 1580 and completely rebuilt it. By acquiring for himself the lordship of the manor, Tanfield deprived the burgesses (the Guild of Merchants) of their traditional rights and made himself extremely unpopular. For 200 years after his death his effigy was burnt in the High Street on Midsummer's Day.

Another interesting memorial is that of *Christopher Kempster* (d. 1715) in the S transept. A master mason, Kempster was one of the men who built the dome of St Paul's Cathedral. Under the mat at the end of the nave before the crossing is a fine brass of 1427, with the figures of George and Alice Spicer.

A memorial of a different kind is the name 'Anthony Sedley prisoner' scratched on the font at the W end of the N aisle. This records an unhappy episode in 1649, when Cromwell rounded up 340 of his rebelling soldiers – the 'Levellers' – and locked them up in the church. Three of them were subsequently shot in the churchyard as an example to the rest – a plaque outside commemorates the event.

The church has some interesting exterior details. These include the splendid three-storey *S porch*, the wool-bale tombs in the churchyard, the Norman *W door* and the decorative arches in the lower (Norman) part of the tower.

Overlooking the Church Green are the *Almshouses* founded in 1457 by Richard, Earl of Warwick, 'the Kingmaker'. (It was near here that Warwick met the future Edward IV to offer him the throne of England.) The almshouses were rebuilt in 1828. On the opposite side of the green is the 16th-c. *Boys' Grammar School*, still used as the school boarding house.

From Church Lane, the High Street

is crossed into Priory Lane. Soon after Sir Lawrence Tanfield's death, the *Priory* became the property of Speaker Lenthall of the Long Parliament. Lenthall enlarged the house and built the chapel, probably to atone for his denial of Charles I. Only a small part of the mansion created by Tanfield and Lenthall remains; it is now the property of an enclosed order of nuns and can be seen only by appointment. Also in Priory Lane is the *Old Rectory, c.* 1700, probably built by Christopher Kempster, and *Falkland Hall*, on the corner, built in 1558.

The long, broad **High Street** runs down to the old bridge over the River Windrush. Nearly every building has a history, many dating in part from before 1500. Of special interest are the *Wesleyan Chapel*, uphill from Priory Lane, a grand Baroque mansion of *c.* 1715, converted into a chapel in 1849; and the medieval *Tolsey*, further up on the corner of Sheep Street, which was used by the Guild of Merchants as a place to meet and collect the tolls for the markets and fairs (now a small museum). There are many good craft and antique shops and several old inns. *The Lamb Inn*, in Sheep Street, is not recorded as an inn before the 18th or 19th c.: the building itself is 15th-c. *The Bay Tree Hotel*, nearby, is 16th-c.

To appreciate Burford fully it is essential to explore its side streets and passages, and perhaps wander along the footpath by the Windrush. See also *Walk 1*, p.18.

½m NE of Burford, across the river, is the small neighbouring village of *Fulbrook*, with the *Church of St James the Great* which retains Norman and 13th-c. features, seen in the porch and doorway, the nave arcade, and the chancel and chancel arch.

2m S on the A361 is the **Cotswold Wildlife Park**, with a wide variety of animals from all over the world, living and often breeding in natural surroundings. With beautiful grounds, adventure playground, restaurant and bar as well as the animals, this makes a marvellous family outing.

Chalford
B4
Village on A419, 4½m SE of Stroud

This little Golden Valley town is built in terraces on the N side of the deep, thickly wooded valley. Many of the narrow streets are too steep for cars. Mills and sheds were built at the bottom, by the fast-flowing stream and the Thames-Severn canal, now derelict. Above them, clinging to the lower slopes of the hillside, are the fine houses built by successful, early 19th-c. clothiers, as well as cottages and Non-Conformist chapels. *Christ Church* was built in 1724 and altered in the 19th c. The font cover and the panelling and ceiling in the sanctuary are by Norman Jewson, the lectern by Peter Waals – both pupils of Ernest Gimson and the Barnsley brothers (see *Sapperton*).

Charlecote Park (NT)
D1
Warwickshire. Historic house off B4086, 4m NE of Stratford-upon-Avon

The Lucy family owned Charlecote Park from the 13th c. until 1945, when it was handed over to the National Trust – though the family still lives in the house. There is a famous legend that in 1583 Shakespeare was prosecuted for poaching deer in the park: deer of the same breed can still be seen grazing in the beautiful parkland that surrounds the house.

Sir Thomas Lucy built the present mellow red brick house *c.*1558, on the site of an older house. This building has been considerably altered, however, much of it rebuilt in the second quarter of the 19th c. Of the original structure, only the attractive *Gatehouse* and the two-storey *porch* still survive. Inside, the *Great Hall*, *Library* and *Dining Room* are richly decorated by Thomas Willemont (1830-40). The rooms contain a fine collection of historical and family portraits. The *Kitchen, c.* 1830, has been kept in its original state.

Among the outbuildings are an early *Brewhouse*, with copper vats and wooden casks (in 1845 it is estimated that 4000 gallons of ale were stored in the cellars under the house), and the *Stables*, with a collection of 19th-c. carriages. There is a good restaurant in the

Above: Gargoyle, St Peter's, Winchcombe   Right: Pittville Pump Room, Cheltenham

Orangery. The *Gardens* were laid out by Capability Brown in 1760.

St Leonard's Church, Charlecote, built 1851-3, contains three fine Lucy tombs of the early 17th c. The tomb of Thomas Lucy (d. 1640) and his wife has behind it a still-life of books and a landscape with Sir Thomas shown on horseback.

Charlton Abbots   C2
Village off A46, 3½m S of Winchcombe

Lying off a quiet country road, this isolated hamlet, high up on the hills, was once owned by the monks of Winchcombe Abbey, who ran a lepers' house here. The tiny 13th-c. *St Martin's Church* was almost completely rebuilt in the 18th c. and restored in 1887. It is hard to find but worth it because of the beautiful views from the churchyard. Look out for a small path by a phone box. The splendid *Manor House* is Elizabethan and Jacobean.

Chastleton House   D2
Oxfordshire. Historic house off A44, 4½m SE of Moreton-in-Marsh

This tall, imposing Jacobean house has suffered no major alteration since it was built in 1603 by Walter Jones. Indeed, many of its furnishings and embroidered tapestries were acquired during the 17th c. by its first owners. Walter Jones was a wealthy wool-stapler and Member of Parliament. He bought the estate of Chastleton for £4000 from the gunpowder-plot conspirator Robert Catesby. Walter's eldest son, Henry, married Ann Fettiplace (see *Swinbrook*, Fettiplace tombs): one of the main bedrooms is named after her, and much of the rich decoration incorporates the Fettiplace arms. It is believed that George Washington was descended from Henry and Anne Jones.

There is an enormous amount to see in this great house: of particular interest are the 17th-c. ornately plastered ceilings in the *Great Chamber*, and the 72-ft *Long Gallery* which was used by the women and children of the house for exercise during the winter months. An amusing piece of furniture here is the 'chamber horse', a chair with a high sprung seat on which the ladies could bounce up and down, simulating the motions of riding. The house is full of rich carved panelling, and has a fine 17th-c. staircase. Chastleton House is still lived in by the Clutton-Brock families, descendants of Walter Jones.

The medieval *Church* is next to the house. The S aisle is full of interesting details: carved Norman capitals, two Baroque wall monuments to members of the Jones family, two brasses (1592 and 1613 – under a carpet) and good 15th-c. tiles. The Jacobean pulpit has wooden panelling like that in Chastleton House. In the field opposite is a delightful arched dovecot, said to be all that remains of Robert Catesby's house.

¾m SE of the church is *Chastleton Barrow Camp*, a circular earthwork with a stone-faced bank, presumably Iron Age.

Chavenage House   B4
Historic house off A433, 1½m NW of Tetbury

This E-shaped Elizabethan manor house was built by Edward Stephens c.1576, probably incorporating an earlier house. His initials can be seen over the porch and on the screen in the hall. Though rather out of the way, the house is well worth a visit.

The finest room in the house is the two-storey *Great Hall*. It has a minstrels' gallery at one end, and two tall mullioned and transomed windows, containing fragments of medieval and 17th-c. heraldic glass. It would originally have been open to the rafters, but now has a flat plaster ceiling. One of the bedrooms is named after Cromwell and another, Ireton: apparently, in 1648 Cromwell and Ireton visited Colonel Nathaniel Stephens, grandson of Edward Stephens, to try to persuade him to vote for Charles I's impeachment. *Cromwell's Room* is hung with a fine tapestry of forest-work, all blues and greens, while *Ireton's Room* has a tapestry showing biblical scenes. The *Ballroom* in the W wing was added in 1905. The owners themselves show visitors round.

Chedworth
C3
Village off A429, 4½m SW of Northleach

This large straggling village is built high up on the steep sides of the valley of a little tributary of the Coln. The stream splashes through the village on its way to the Coln below, and some of the houses are buttressed to prevent them sliding down the slope. The late Norman *St Andrew's Church* has a splendid Perpendicular S façade, with windows extending almost from ground to parapet and a fine array of carved bosses and gargoyles below the parapet. The wineglass-shaped pulpit is one of the best 15th-c. carved stone pulpits in the Cotswolds.

Chedworth Roman Villa is directly accessible by car from the Fossebridge-Yanworth-Withington road. The energetic might prefer the walk (2m) through Chedworth Woods: leave Chedworth on the Yanworth road, and the footpath to the Roman Villa is signposted to the left. At the top of the first field follow the path round to the right and down into the woods. Set at the head of a wooded valley, the villa was excavated in 1864-6, and is the most completely exposed of any in the W of England. Lord Eldon, who owned the site at the time, built the custodian's house, the museum, and the protective coverings over the remains. The entire floor plan of the villa, including the extensive bath-houses, can be traced, and some beautiful mosaics survive. The small finds from the site are housed in the museum.

SE of Chedworth near the A429 is the *Denfurlong Farm Trail*. Here, visitors can study a working dairy farm and take themselves on self-conducted tours, using audio-visual aids, which explain crop rotation and wild-life conservation.

Cheltenham
B3
Town 8m NE of Gloucester, 15m NW of Cirencester. Pop: 86,000. Events: International Festival of Music (1st fortnight Jul), Horse Show (Jul), Cricket Festival (Aug), Festival of Music, Speech, Drama & Dancing (mid Oct). EC Wed MD Thur. Inf: Tel (0242) 22878

In the 17th c. Cheltenham was a small market town with a population of perhaps 350 families. It was still the town described by John Leland in his *Itinerary*: 'a long towne havynge a Market. There is a brook on the South Syde of the Towne.' The town's main livelihood was then the illegal cultivation of tobacco. The only medieval building that survives today is the parish Church of St Mary's.

In 1718 a spring was discovered on the site of what is now the Princess Hall (a part of the Ladies' College). Captain Henry Skillicorne, one of the owners of the site, was soon to exploit the medicinal properties of the waters, building the first Spa in 1738. The visit of George III and his family in 1788 (described by Fanny Burney in her *Diary*) established the fame of the waters: in 1816 they received a further boost when the Duke of Wellington, whose liver complaint had been cured by a sample, opened an Assembly Room.

The growing popularity of the resort provided a great momentum for building. One of the earliest developments was the Lansdown Estate, designed by the architect J.B. Papworth; before this was completed the Member of Parliament, Joseph Pitt, had begun the Pittville Estate. These were the first in a series of ambitious projects that created the beautiful Regency town of Cheltenham.

By the time the waters had ceased to attract visitors, Cheltenham had become a prosperous, middle-class town, and a retirement area for those returning from India and the colonies. Good educational establishments were a priority for the privileged and the first – the Cheltenham College for Boys – was built in 1841-3. Next came the Ladies' College, founded in 1854, developed to its present importance by Miss Dorothea Beale, who was its headmistress from 1858 for 50 years.

Church-building was another priority for a pious, straight-laced community. 'There are great spiritual advantages to be had in the town,' George Eliot commented in *Middlemarch*. The new churches, in the Gothic Revival style, are of no great merit.

Cheltenham's real interest lies in her splendid Regency squares and houses, which can be appreciated in a short walking tour. Best starting point is the **Promenade**, a wide elegant street given up to fashionable shops on the E side but with a fine classical terrace on the W. Originally private houses, the terrace is now used for municipal offices, which include the Tourist Information Centre. At the N end of the Promenade (left out of the Tourist Office) the High Street is joined. Going left along it, a passage on the left leads to the small square in which stands the only surviving building of medieval Cheltenham, **St Mary's Parish Church**.

Up to the Dissolution this building, originally 12th-c., belonged to Cirencester Abbey. The windows are particularly fine, with good Victorian stained glass best appreciated in the evening light. Most remarkable is the rose window in the N transept, representing the Wheel of St Catherine, with its original 14th-c. tracery. Much of the church, including the tower, is also 14th-c. There are several interesting monuments, including an early 16th-c. brass to William Grevil, his wife and children, to the left of the altar, and a long epitaph to the Skillicorne family behind the pulpit which is almost a history of the town's origins.

In the churchyard there is a stone bearing this verse:

Here lie I with my two daughters
Who died from drinking Cheltenham waters.
If we had stuck to Epsom salts,
We wouldn't be lying in these damp vaults.

The authenticity of this is uncertain.

Well Walk leads S out of the churchyard to Clarence Street. To the left, on the opposite side of Clarence Street, Crescent Place leads to Royal Crescent, which has some of the town's finest Regency buildings. This is a diversion: the tour continues right up Clarence Street to the **Museum, Art Gallery and Library** with its collection of 17th-c. Dutch paintings and numerous items of local history. A special feature of the museum is the Edward Wilson Collection, devoted to the explorer. Opposite the museum, St George's Place leads down to St George's Road. Turning left, the oldest part of the *Cheltenham Ladies' College* is on the corner of St George's Road and Montpellier Street. Continuing E, the Promenade is rejoined. (Note, at this end, the *statue* of Edward Wilson.)

From here a Regency terrace climbs to a view of Imperial Square and Gardens, with the Town Hall on the N and the majestic colonnaded *Queen's Hotel* (1838) on the S. Proceeding S, Montpellier Avenue joins Montpellier Walk, a splendid row of shops with fine cast-iron work over the facias and interposed caryatid figures. At the end of the Walk is the Regency *Rotunda*, now Lloyds Bank, but built as Montpellier Spa. At this point a number of fine Regency streets branch off in different directions, the most notable Lansdown Crescent and Suffolk Square.

The route of the tour is continued along Montpellier Terrace, at the foot of Montpellier Gardens. Shortly on the right is Suffolk Parade, the main area in the town for antique shops; next on the left is Montpellier Parade, which leads back to Imperial Square (left at the end and right into Trafalgar Street, left again into the square). The *Town Hall* on the N side of the square was built in 1902-3 to replace the Assembly Rooms, demolished at that time, as a social centre. Here visitors may sample Cheltenham's famous waters.

Holst Birthplace Museum Worth visiting at No 4 Clarence Road is the house where the composer Gustav Holst (1874-1934) was born. In addition to the Holst memorabilia, there are rooms furnished in the style of the Regency and Victorian periods.

Pittville Park The Evesham Road runs through these charming gardens on the N side of Cheltenham, an ornament to the estate developed by Joseph Pitt in the 1820s. Overlooking the gardens and accessible from the road is the **Pittville Pump Room**, built by John Forbes (1825-30) as the showplace of Cheltenham Spa for the then prodigious

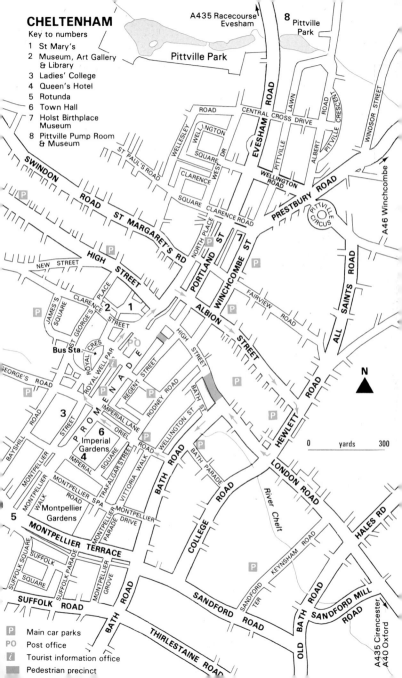

sum of £40,000. With its Ionic colonnade, *Great Hall* and domed gallery it is Cheltenham's most spectacular Regency building. Spa water may still be drunk from the original fountain in the hall. Also in the building is the *Pittville Pump Room Museum*, which contains a visual presentation of the town's history from the late 18th c. and an exhibition of period costumes.

Chipping Campden   C2

Small town on B4081/B4035, 7m NW of Moreton-in-Marsh. Event: Dover's Games (Fri & Sat after Spring Bank Hol Mon). EC Thur, Sat. Inf: Tel (0386) 840289

Built in the hollow beneath Dover's Hill, by the time of Domesday the manor of Campden had about 300 inhabitants, and as early as 1247 it had weekly markets ('Chipping' means 'Market') and three annual fair days. It was during the 14th c. that it became one of the chief collecting points and markets for the wool trade, and it was the immensely wealthy wool merchants who built up the great Perpendicular church and the splendid houses that give the town its unique character. William Grevel has been considered the town's greatest benefactor: he died in 1401 and his memorial brass in the church describes him as 'the flower of the wool merchants of all England'.

St James's Church, originally Norman, owes its impression of harmony and unity to the 15th-c. rebuilding. The great W tower is possibly the finest of any Cotswold church. The nave of *c.* 1488, was almost certainly built by the master mason responsible for the nave at Northleach.

Set into the chancel floor are the brasses of William Grevel and his wife and other wool merchants, including William Gibbys (d. 1484) with his three wives and 13 children. To the right of the chancel is the *Gainsborough Chapel*, with recumbent effigies of Sir Baptist Hicks, first Viscount Campden (d. 1629) and his wife in their state robes; there are also larger than life-sized alabaster figures representing their daughter Juliana and her husband Sir Edward Noel dressed in their shrouds.

Amongst the other monuments is a recumbent effigy of Sir Thomas Smythe (d. 1593) to the left of the altar, with his two wives and children. Lord of the Manor of Campden, Sir Thomas was the first Governor of the East India Company.

The church also contains a 15th-c. velvet cope, embroidered with powdered coronets and the figures of saints, and a complete set of late 15th-c. altar cloths. The Jacobean pulpit and 15th-c. lectern were donated by Sir Baptist Hicks (he also contributed many fine buildings to the town, described below).

From a door by the entrance at the SW corner of the church steps lead up into a little tower (14th-c.) beside the S porch. Here is the *Muniment Room*, once a schoolroom and now a treasury of church documents.

Adjacent to the churchyard are the lodges and gateway of the great mansion, *Old Campden House*, built by Sir Baptist Hicks in 1613. The house was burnt down in the Civil War. Two pavilions and a small almonry building are the only other remains. On the opposite side of Church Street are Sir Baptist's *Almshouses*, built in the shape of the letter 'I' from the initial of the Latin version of James I's name.

The wide, curving **High Street**, called by G.M. Trevelyan 'the most beautiful village street in England' has fine buildings of many periods. The oldest are *Grevel House*, opposite Church Street, built by William Grevel at the end of the 14th c., and the *Woolstaplers' Hall*, opposite, built at about the same time for Robert Calf, another rich wool merchant. A small museum here has a mixed collection including medical and photographic equipment. Next to the Woolstaplers' Hall is *Bedfont House*, built by master mason Thomas Woodward, the finest 18th-c. house in the street. Next to that is Sherborn House with the *Campden Car Collection* of historic cars from 1927-63.

On an island in the middle of the street is **Market Hall**, built in 1627 by

Sir Baptist Hicks to house the poultry, butter and cheese market. It is now the property of the National Trust.

As there were no suitable streams to power mills, the town declined in importance in the 18th and 19th c., but in 1902 C.R. Ashbee, a follower of Ruskin and William Morris, brought his Guild of Handicrafts here, and the town has been a thriving centre for arts and crafts ever since. The Campden Trust, formed in 1929, has bought and restored houses and has been extremely successful in preserving Campden's architecture. Even the council houses are built of Cotswold stone. Chipping Campden now marks the beginning of the *Cotswold Way*.

1m NW of the village is *Dover's Hill*, named after Captain Robert Dover, who inaugurated the Cotswold Games (also known as the 'Cotswold Olympicks' or ' Dover's Games') *c.* 1612. James I approved of the venture and even gave Dover an old suit of his, with hat and feather, to wear when he opened the games. Wrestling, leaping, 'pitching the bar', horse-racing, bullbaiting, coursing and cock-fighting were amongst the most popular sports, as well as the peculiarly Cotswold sport of shin-kicking. Eventually, in 1852, the games were ended because of the disorderly mobs that used to come down from the Midlands. Revived for the Festival of Britain, they are now a more modest affair – but still include shin-kicking. Held on the Friday after the Spring Bank Holiday, they are followed next day by the Scuttlebrook Wake Fair.

Dover's Hill is now National Trust property. On the edge of the Scarp overlooking the Vale of Evesham, it offers fine views and good walking.

Chipping Norton D2

Oxfordshire. Small town on A44, 9m SE of Moreton-in-Marsh. EC Thur MD Wed. Inf: Tel (0608) 41320

This ancient market town is the highest town in Oxfordshire. The wide High Street and Market Place run into each other, thus providing a large open space

for the horse fairs that were held here in the Middle Ages (the markets that are held here today occupy only a fraction of this space). Chipping Norton was once an important wool town, and its prosperity seems to have continued into the 17th and 18th c.

Though traces of earlier work remain, **St Mary's Church** is mainly Perpendicular. The nave was rebuilt *c.* 1485, purportedly at the expense of John Ashfield, a wool merchant. Slender pillars, unbroken by capitals, support the timber roof, while the clerestory windows provide an almost continuous band of glazing above the nave. There is a seven-light window over the chancel arch, and a striking Decorated window filling the entire E end of the S aisle, which is said to have been taken from Bruern Abbey. The church has a rare hexagonal *porch*, with buttresses and gargoyles outside and fine vaulting and bosses carved as grinning devils inside. There are several 15th- and early 16th-c. brasses in the church, though they have unfortunately been taken up and set on wooden panels. There are also two good 16th-c. tombs with alabaster effigies.

A row of *Almshouses*, dated 1640, leads from the church to the *High Street*. Here and in the *Market Place* are a good many 17th-, 18th- and 19th-c. inns and shops. The Market Place has the 19th-c. *Town Hall* at one end and the 16th-c. *Guildhall* at the other.

Cirencester C4

Town 15m S of Cheltenham. Pop: 14,800. Events: Carnival (1st Sat in Jul). EC Thur MD Mon, Fri. Inf: Tel (0285) 4180

Cirencester today is a bustling little town, serving the locality with its markets and shops: for tourists it is one of the most attractive centres in the Cotswolds. Its modern image tends to obscure its historical importance: in Roman times Corinium Dobunnorum was, after London, the second largest town in Britain. It was founded in 75AD, probably because of its proximity to the local tribe of the Dobunni at Bagendon, who were friendly to the Roman conquerors. By the 2nd c. AD

Overleaf: Cirencester House and Park

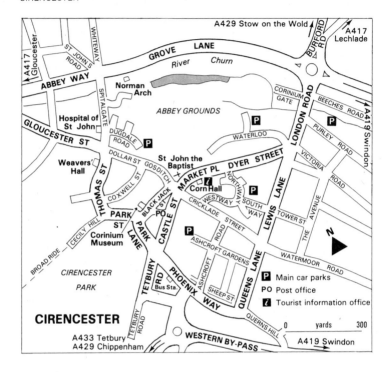

CIRENCESTER

A433 Tetbury
A429 Chippenham

P Main car parks
PO Post office
i Tourist information office

0   yards   300

it had developed into a town of considerable size. Its walls, 8ft thick and 2m round, enclosed an area of 240 acres, and the town stood on the crossroads of three major trade routes, including the Fosse Way. From relics and modern reconstructions (on display in the Corinium Museum) it is evident that this was a town of considerable elegance and sophistication, of colonnaded streets and large villas with beautiful mosaic floors. To the W of the town, at the end of Querns Lane, are the remains of the *Amphitheatre*, now only grassy banks some 20ft high enclosing an area of level ground. Corinium flourished until the 6th c. when the Saxons defeated the Britons of Mercia and burnt the town to the ground.

Cirencester's second period of greatness was in the Middle Ages, when it became the largest wool market in England. The parish **Church of St John the Baptist** in the Market Place is the finest of the 'wool' churches, and one of the largest parish churches in England, with the dimensions of a small cathedral. The earliest work in the church dates from the 12th and 13th c., but it was at the beginning of the 15th c. that the rebuilding began that was to make the church the magnificent building it is today. From this period date the tower and the Trinity and Lady Chapels. The porch (1490) and the vaulting of St Catherine's Chapel (1508) were later. The final stage of the rebuilding came in the early 16th c., when the 13th-c. nave was replaced by a splendid Tudor one, 15ft higher than its predecessor, with a continuous clerestory row of four-light windows.

The *S porch* – after the nave the most impressive part of the church – has three storeys with three lofty oriel windows and splendid fan vaulting. For a while the upper part was used as a council chamber, and after the Dissolution as Town Hall. Inside the church the tall Perpendicular *nave* can be admired in all its glory: the donors who were responsible for its enlargement – wool merchants, landowners, etc., are commemorated by stone angels above the piers, bearing their family badges. Two features of interest in the nave are the 15th-c. 'wine-glass' pulpit, one of the few pre-Reformation pulpits remaining in Gloucestershire, and the Boleyn Cup (given by Henry VIII to Anne Boleyn two years before her execution) to the right of the chancel arch. Off the N aisle of the church is the highly-decorated *Trinity Chapel*, built by the Weavers Company, which contains some fine 15th-c. memorial brasses. The *Lady Chapel*, at the end of the aisle next to it, also has brasses and a splendid monument to Humfry Bridges (d. 1598) and his wife. *St Catherine's Chapel*, next to the Lady Chapel, has superb fan vaulting. In the wall between the two chapels there survives a small Romanesque arch of *c*. 1120.

The church has a peal of 12 bells, the oldest in the country. The building was restored by Sir George Gilbert Scott in 1865-7.

The Market Place is a good starting point for a walking tour of the town. Opposite the church, to the left, is the *Corn Hall* (1862) incorporating the Tourist Office and a weekly antiques market: next to it *The King's Head* with its 18th-c. façade. Down Dyer Street to the E is the 17th-c. *Bear Inn*, a timber-framed building with overhanging storeys.

In the other direction, from the W end of the church, Black Jack Street leads to Park Street. On the right is the **Corinium Museum**, which houses one of Britain's most impressive Roman collections. Well-preserved mosaic pavements are incorporated in replicas of the rooms in which they stood, and there are numerous other relics and reconstructions.

On the left of Park Street is the entrance to the mansion of **Cirencester Park**, hidden behind a 30ft yew hedge. Seat of the Earl Bathurst, the mansion was built in 1714-18. The grounds, which cover 3000 acres, are approached by a separate gate at the top of Cecily Hill on the left. They were laid out by the first Earl Bathurst with the help of the poet Alexander Pope, whose summerhouse retreat, 'Pope's Seat' can still be seen. The *Broad Ride* (a continuation of Cecily Hill) stretches for 5m to Sapperton and is one of the longest avenues in England.

From the bottom of Cecily Hill turn left into Thomas Street, which has, to the left, a diversion to an attractive riverside walk. On the right is *Coxwell Street*, with many attractive old houses: note *Coxwell Court*, now being restored, a fascinating 17th-c. house with 18th-c. additions and, inside, Queen Anne panelled rooms. At the top of Coxwell Street to the left is Dollar Street, with its bow-windowed shops (some 17th-c.). Proceeding along it, Thomas Street is rejoined, with (at the top) the *Weavers' Hall*, founded in 1425 as a hostel for poor weavers.

Turning right from Dollar Street into Spitalgate Lane, the Norman-Transitional arcade of *St John's Hospital* may be seen on the left. Founded by Henry I, it is now beautifully restored. At the end of Spitalgate turn right into Grove Lane, and, a little way along on the right, note the Norman *Abbey Gate* – all that survives of Cirencester's 12th-c. Abbey. Endowed by Henry I, the Abbey was extremely rich and the Abbot not only had a seat in Parliament but coined his own money. At the Dissolution the Abbey was demolished. Passing through the gate, a return route can be made via the Abbey Grounds to the Market Place, using the church tower as a guide.

3m SW of the town at Kemble is the **Smerrill Farm Museum**, where a typical Cotswold farmyard has been converted into a display of farm equipment, butter and cheese making, etc.

Market Hall, Chipping Campden

Above: St James's, Chipping Campden   Right: Fettiplace Monuments, Swinbrook

Cleeve Common B2

High ground on the Cotswold Edge NE of Cheltenham

On the Cheltenham-Winchcombe road (A46) at Cleeve Hill village, a layby offers convenient parking for the highest point of Cleeve Common (another approach is by footpath from Southam). At 1083ft the *Beacon* is the highest point in the Cotswolds. A dial shows exactly what may be seen on a clear day: Tewkesbury in one direction and Gloucester in another.

Various prehistoric remains can be seen in the area. *The Ring*, a circular enclosure with bank and ditch, was possibly an ancient ritual circle preceding those made of upright stones. To the S is an Iron Age British *fort*, and below that a great rough-hewn stone known as *Huddlestone's Rock*. 2m to the E is **Belas Knap*.

These bleak, open wolds are now partly a golf course, but give an idea of what the Cotswolds must have been like before the Enclosure Acts and the cultivation of the old sheep runs.

Coates B4

Village off A419, 3m SW of Cirencester

The main attraction is not the village but the canal which lies beyond it, to the SW. Leaving Coates by the Tarlton road, watch out for an inn sign on the right, just after a railway bridge. The drive here leads to *The Tunnel House Inn*, an 18th-c. hostelry built for the Thames-Severn canal bargees, and now a pleasant place for lunch or a drink. A short climb down from the pub is the entrance to the 2½m-long Sapperton Tunnel: the arch is ornate, with Doric columns.

In Coates village there is a Norman church, *St Matthew's*, with a Norman S doorway, three-bay Transitional arcade, and early Perpendicular tower; it was restored in 1861. Many of the cottages were built in the 18th c. for canal maintenance men. In a meadow near *Trewsbury House* to the S is *Thames Head*, one of the two disputed sources of the River Thames (see also **Coberley*). A footpath leads to the spot from the village (see *Walk 7*, p.20).

Coberley B3

Village off A435, 4½m S of Cheltenham

There is not much to the village except **St Giles' Church** and a handful of buildings round it, but the church itself is fascinating. Approached through the arched doorway of a farm, it is hardly visible from the road. It has a Perpendicular tower, and the S porch and S chapel date from *c.* 1340, but the nave and chancel were rebuilt in 1870 – very successfully. The *S Chapel* contains large effigies of a knight and his lady, thought to be Sir Thomas Berkeley, who fought at Crecy, and Lady Joan, whose second husband was Sir William Whittington, father of Dick Whittington, three times Lord Mayor of London. They lived at Coberley Hall, which had long been the home of the Berkeleys; nothing remains of it now, as it was pulled down in the 18th c. The chapel also contains a much smaller effigy of a girl – perhaps a daughter – and another of a young man in civilian dress. In the sanctuary is a heart-burial monument, the only one in the Cotswolds. It is thought to represent Sir Giles Berkeley, father of Sir Thomas; he was buried at Little Malvern in 1295 but his heart was brought back to Coberley. His favourite horse, Leonard, is buried in the churchyard. The Berkeley arms are carved on the buttresses of the church tower. Note also the gargoyles on the tower.

1m N of Coberley is *Seven Springs*, the second disputed source of the Thames (see also **Coates*). Seven tiny springs emerge from a bank to form a little stream, the infant Churn: not, it must be admitted, a very impressive sight. As this source is further from the Churn's junction with the Thames at Cricklade than Thames Head, it is argued that the Churn is in fact the Thames.

Colesbourne B3

Village on A435, 6m SE of Cheltenham, 9m NW of Cirencester

Colesbourne Park is famous for its many rare trees from all over the world, planted last century by Henry Elwes, author of *The Trees of Britain*. The

19th-c. mansion has mostly been demolished. The greatest treasure of the little church nearby – St James – is the 15th-c. chalice-shaped pulpit on a tall, fluted octagonal stem. There is also some good Victorian needlework. 1m to the N is *Norbury Iron Age Fort*.

Coln Rogers, Coln St Aldwyns and Coln St Dennis
C3

Villages near Bibury: Coln Rogers and Coln St Dennis respectively 3½m and 4½m NW (off A429); Coln St Aldwyns 2m SE (off A433)

The little village of **Coln St Dennis** is the furthest upstream of these three Coln Valley villages. The Norman *St James' Church* is almost as it was built, though the arches of the central tower have sagged slightly: from the outside the whole church appears to bow outwards. ½m to the W, on the other side of the A429, is *The Fossebridge Hotel*, where lunch can be eaten on a lawn beside the Coln.

Coln Rogers, another very small village, is named after a Norman knight called Roger of Gloucester, who gave Coln Rogers to the Abbey of Gloucester in 1150. The nave and chancel of the Saxon *St Andrew's Church* have survived almost intact, except that the windows have been enlarged, the chancel lengthened, and a tower built in the nave. 1½m to the SW is the 300ft *Colnpen Long Barrow* and a group of four or five round barrows.

Coln St Aldwyns, the largest of the three villages, is built on a steep hillside, with an old mill at the bottom down by the river and the church at the top. Sir Michael Hicks-Beach, then Chancellor of the Exchequer and later the first Lord St Aldwyn, altered and enlarged the 16th-c. gabled *Manor House* in 1896. The present Lord St Aldwyn lives at Williamstrip Park (see *Hatherop*). The Norman *Church of St John the Baptist* is beautifully situated, with a fine tower, but it was over-restored in 1853 and the inside is rather dull. John Keble's father was vicar here 1782-1835, and John Keble himself was curate for the last ten years; the two stained glass windows in the church over the altar were erected in 1910 as a memorial to them both. They lived at *Fairford* as there was not then a suitable vicarage in the village. *The New Inn* serves an excellent pub lunch.

Compton Abdale
C3

Village off A40, 4m NW of Northleach

This small village is situated in a deep well-shaded valley, with its *Church* built on a slope overlooking the cross-roads. The Perpendicular tower has four pinnacles in the shape of heraldic beasts and on the offsets are *couchant* animals. A stream gushes out of the mouth of a stone crocodile and runs down a paved bed at the side of the village street.

Compton Wynyates
D1

Warwickshire. Historic house 7m NE of Shipston-on-Stour

Built by Sir William Compton in the early 16th c., the house was once known as 'Compton-in-the-Hole' on account of its low-lying position in the hollow of the hills. The name 'Wyn Yates' (vineyards) relates to a time when these slopes were covered in vines.

The Comptons were much in favour with the Tudors and Stuarts and many kings and queens including Henry VIII and Catherine of Aragon, Elizabeth I and Charles I stayed here. Pevsner calls Compton 'the most perfect picture-book house of the early Tudor decades'. Although the building is now the private residence of the Marquis of Northampton and not open to the public, it is worth going to the top of the drive for a view of the rambling, brick-built mansion with its gables, towers and chimneys. The grounds include a 17th-c. *Chapel*.

Condicote
C2

Village off B4077, 4m NW of Stow-on-the-Wold

The centre of this high N Cotswold village is a rough green enclosed by dry-stone walling, with a 17th- or 18th-c. farmhouse at each corner and a 14th-c. wayside cross at the W end. The 12th-c. *St Nicholas' Church* overlooks the green. It was very over-restored in 1888, and the walls scraped of plaster, but a considerable amount of Norman work remains. The Norman *S door*, in particular, is richly ornamented.

Cooper's Hill
B3
5½m SW of Cheltenham, to S of the A46

It is here that the ancient ceremony of cheese-rolling takes place each year. As it originally took place at midsummer, it seems likely that the rolled cheeses symbolised the sun, the idea being to arrest the shortening of the days and to ensure the sun's return the following year. In the past, the ceremony included maypole dancing, and, at some time in the 19th c., it also included pulling faces through a horse collar (which is still done at festivals in the Lake District), as well as dancing and wrestling for the ribbons and belt worn by the master of ceremonies. The present festival takes place on Spring Bank Holiday Monday, when the contestants chase 7lb cheeses down the 200yd, 1:1 slope, the winner keeping the cheese.

Cooper's Hill is now a nature reserve of about 137 acres, with the longest nature trail in the Cotswolds. On a fine day one can see from Severn Bridge in the S to the Malverns and Bredon Hill in the N, with the Sugar Loaf and Black Mountains of Wales in the W. The Cotswold Way footpath passes the base of the famous cheese-rolling slope.

Cowley
B3
Village off A435, 5m S of Cheltenham

The second village on the River Churn after Coberley. The river is diverted into the terraced grounds of *Cowley Manor* to make ornamental lakes and cascades. Here many rare birds and plants find a sanctuary – exotic vegetation can be seen in the clear water of the lake directly below the house. The rather square manor house was completely rebuilt in 1855-60, in the Italian style, and further enlarged at the end of the 19th c. It is now used by Gloucestershire County Council as a centre for cultural activities and adult education. Sadly, these enchanting gardens are not open to the public, but there is a good view of them from the road that runs round the far side. Further along this road is *The Green Dragon Inn*, where lunch can be eaten outside, overlooking woods and valleys and the grounds of Cowley Manor. Children are welcome.

The village church, *St Mary's*, is just inside the manor grounds. It is rather gloomy inside, but note the decorated Norman font and the early 14th-c. recumbent effigy of a priest in Eucharistic vestments in the chancel.

Cranham
B3
Village off A46, 7m NE of Stroud, 7m SW of Cheltenham. Event: Feast & Ox Roast (2nd weekend Aug)

This scattered hillside village lies in the midst of beechwoods but has a conspicuous church, *St James's*, overlooking Cranham Common. From the large churchyard, with its clipped yews lining the path to the church, there are fine views of the woods and valleys all around. The church is mainly 15th-c., though much altered in the late 19th c. The Perpendicular tower has gargoyles and two pairs of one-handed sheep shears carved on it – which suggests that wool merchants provided the funds for its building. The church possesses a pre-Reformation screen, a rare thing in the Cotswolds as they were mostly destroyed by Bishop Hooper. Note also the lively Baroque painted stone monument to the Rev Obadiah Done (died 1738, Rector of Cranham for 51 years), with *putti* holding wooden palms and trumpets.

Cranham Feast and Ox Roast, held at Overton Farm in August, is a popular local event, with people dressed in medieval costume.

1m to the E is *Buckle Wood*, where a 150ft-long barrow containing 20 human skeletons was found. *Cooper's Hill* and *Witcombe Roman Villa* (*Great Witcombe*) are both within easy reach.

Crickley Hill Country Park
B3
Country park 3m S of Cheltenham, at junction of A417 and A436 (by *Air Balloon* public house)

This area was recently scheduled as a site of Special Scientific Interest and a Cotswold Area of Outstanding Beauty; it is now managed by the National Trust and Gloucestershire County Council. Three specific interest trails have been marked: ecological, geological, archaeological. There is also a family trail suitable for the disabled and people with young children. There is an

Iron Age *fort* at the top of the hill, and excavations continue for six weeks every summer. It can be visited at any time during this period, but for two days in August there are guides who will show interested visitors round and explain what is being done. Crickley Hill has some of the best viewpoints of the Cotswolds.

Daglingworth B3

Village off A417, 3m NW of Cirencester

Daglingworth has an exceptionally interesting church, sited well above the rest of the village. Saxon in origin, and consolidated by the Normans, *Holy Rood Church* was drastically reconstructed in 1845-50. A good deal of Saxon work survives, however, including the *S doorway* and the sundial above it (the door itself is 15th-c.). During the 19th-c. reconstruction three Saxon carved panels, representing the Crucifixion, St Peter with his key, and Our Lord enthroned, were discovered, facing inwards, in the chancel arch; they are now in the nave and N aisle. They are thought to have been walled up since before the Norman Conquest, and as a result are extremely well preserved. By contrast the Saxon stone crucifix near the pulpit, which was removed from the outer E wall, is much weathered. The church also contains a carved Roman panel, inscribed to the Mother-goddess, in the vestry wall.

The rather attractive square house next to the church is *Daglingworth House*, built in the early 19th c.

Daneway House see *Sapperton*

Daylesford D2

Village off A436, 3½m E of Stow-on-the-Wold

Macaulay tells how, when seven years old, Warren Hastings lay on a river bank and swore to recover his ancestors' estates and become Hastings of Daylesford. He succeeded, and in 1787 S.P. Cockerell (later the builder of Sezincote) began to build Daylesford House for him. Unfortunately it is not visible from any road.

In 1816 Hastings took down the original medieval *St Peter's Church* and re-

built it, but in 1860 it was rebuilt again, in wonderfully ornate Victorian Gothic style. It has a mass of rich carving, marbles and mosaics all over the walls of the sanctuary, and superb, brilliantly coloured stained glass throughout. On the N wall of the nave is a tablet, commissioned by Warren Hastings in 1816, recording the history of the church, and next to it are tablets to Hastings and his wife. Just E of the church is the splendid Coade stone monument over Hastings' grave, with the simple inscription 'Warren Hastings 1818'.

Devil's Chimney see *Leckhampton*

Didbrook C2

Village off A46, 3m NE of Winchcombe

St George's Church is wholly Perpendicular in style, having been completely rebuilt *c.* 1475 by Abbot Whitchurch of Hailes, supposedly because the former church had been the scene of the murder of some Lancastrian refugees from Tewkesbury. The most striking feature is the way the tower is carried on three open arches within the nave. The interior was completely panelled in the 18th c., but now only the wooden panelling on the Georgian chancel arch remains. A panel of 15th-c. glass in the E window shows two angels praying, presumably for the soul of Abbot Whitchurch, whose name is mentioned in the inscription. Most of the cottages in the village are partly stone and partly timber-framed; Nos 62 and 63 are a very old example of 'cruck' construction, exposed at one end.

Donnington D2

Village off A429, 2m N of Stow-on-the-Wold

Donnington consists only of a few 17th- and 18th-c. cottages and a remodelled 18th-c. *Manor House*, but it is attractively situated, in open, upland country, with fine views over the Evenlode Valley.

2m to the W, 1m N of Upper Swell is *Donnington Brewery*. There was a mill here in the 14th c., and by 1827 when the Arkells bought it there were three mills, a bakehouse and a malthouse. The independent brewery, still owned by the Arkell family, now brews 'real ale' for the local Donnington houses. The lake or millpond on which it stands affords a haven for many different species of water-birds, brought here by the owners, who have provided islands, nesting places and shelters for them. The lake surrounded by hills, the handful of stone cottages, and the numerous and noisy water-birds make this a truly delightful spot. Though it is not open to the public, the owners are prepared to receive visitors by appointment.

Dowdeswell B3
Village off A40, 3m SE of Cheltenham

Situated in a wooded valley at the edge of the Cotswold Scarp, the village is on the other side of the main road from the lake-like Dowdeswell Reservoir. The little *St Michael's Church*, Norman in origin, has a stone spire and two 19th-c. galleries, both entered by private external doors and staircases; one belonged to the manor, the other to the rectory. The most notable of the church's many monuments are a brass of a priest in processional garments, *c.* 1520, at the foot of the altar steps (the carpet has to be lifted), and a marble monument to William Rogers (d. 1734). Next to the church is a group of Tudor farm buildings, including a dovecote built over a delightful half-timbered arch. The 19th-c. *Dowdeswell Court* is now a school.

Driffield C4
Village off A419, 4m SE of Cirencester

The medieval *St Mary's Church* was completely rebuilt by the first Lord Coleraine in 1734 and restored (by Butterfield) in 1863. Inside are a number of tablets to the Hanger family. One reads: 'Here lieth in expectation of the last day, Gabriel Hanger, Lord Coleraine, what manner of man he was, that day will disclose', and another says of George Hanger, a Regency rake, that he was 'a practical Christian as far as his frail nature did allow him so to be'. This Lord Coleraine, who died in 1824, sold the material of his mansion at Driffield by auction in 1803, perhaps to pay his gambling debts. The mansion, next to the church, was later demolished.

Duntisbourne Abbots, Duntisbourne Leer, Middle Duntisbourne, and Duntisbourne Rouse B3
Villages off A417, respectively 5½, 5, 4 and 3½m NW of Cirencester

Of these four villages – or hamlets – on the Duntisbourne Brook, **Duntisbourne Abbots** is the largest. Once a possession of the Abbey of Gloucester, it is a pretty village, mostly built round a steeply sloping green. The Norman *St Peter's Church*, at the top of the green, is dark and over-restored. 1m to the N is *Cotswold Farm*, a 17th-c. farmhouse altered and enlarged by Sidney Barnsley in 1926. The library has a modelled plaster ceiling by Norman Jewson, and the stained glass window in the dining room is by Burne-Jones.

Barely ½m downstream is the hamlet of **Duntisbourne Leer**, once owned by the Abbey of Lire in Normandy. Here a farmhouse and a few cottages are built round a ford. ¾m to the SW is a 120ft-long chambered *long barrow*, with the *Hoar Stone* at one end. And 1m further downstream, **Middle Duntisbourne** again consists of some cottages and farm buildings gathered round a ford.

Duntisbourne Rouse is the last Duntisbourne, named after the Rouse family. The church, **St Michael's**, stands on such a steep slope that a crypt has been built beneath the chancel. The nave is probably Saxon, the chancel and crypt, early Norman, and the little saddleback tower, Perpendicular. Inside, there are some interesting furnishings: real box pews, Jacobean pulpit, and 15th- or 16th-c. choir stalls with misericords with grotesque heads.

Dursley A4
Small town on B4066, 10m SW of Stroud

This pleasant small town, located in a sheltered situation in the wooded Cam Valley, was for centuries, as the manor of Dursley, under the patronage of the Berkeley family. By the 15th c. it was one of the Cotswolds' most important wool and cloth towns and home of many immigrant French and Flemish weavers. Now devoted to other industries, and a commuter satellite of Bristol, Dursley is very much a modern town, but retains a number of good Georgian houses.

There are only two earlier buildings of any significance. On an island site at the central crossroads of the town, the *Market House* (1738) is a grandiose building set on arches, with a statue of Queen Anne on the E front. Opposite is *St James's Church*, dominated by its huge tower. The church, originally 12th c., was rebuilt in the 14th, but much of it is now considerably later. The tower was rebuilt in 1709 in the Gothic style after being ruined by the collapse of a steeple added to it 10 years previously.

1m NW is *Stinchmore Hill*, good walking country with fine views of the Berkeley Vale, particularly from Drakestone Point. At Blanchworth Farm, near Stinchcombe Village, is the **Cider Mill Gallery**, where traditional cider-making with a horse-drawn mill can be seen in the autumn (also pottery, art gallery and craft shops).

Eastleach Martin,
Eastleach Turville
D3
Villages off A417 or A361, 4m NE of Fairford

Facing each other across the River Leach, their two churches only a stone's throw apart, the two Eastleaches were originally two separate manors with their own churches. **Eastleach Turville** is the bigger of the two, with an attractive-looking pub, *The Victoria Inn*, at the top of a grassy bank. *St Andrew's Church* has a tiny early 14th-c. saddleback tower, a carved tympanum of Christ in Majesty supported by angels over the S doorway, *c.* 1130, and a roof of elm cut from the parish in 1906. The 13th-c. chancel has an elegant E wall, with triple lancets under richly moulded arches.

There is a road bridge between Eastleach Turville and **Eastleach Martin** (better known as Bouthrop), but the pleasantest way to get from one to the other is to use the footbridge of huge flat stones, known as *Keble's Bridge* (probably in honour of the Keble family who held the manor of Eastleach Turville for five generations, and not for John Keble, who was non-resident

curate here immediately after his ordination in 1815). Once over the bridge a short walk along the river takes the visitor to Eastleach Martin's *Church of St Michael and St Martin*, which is both smaller and older than that of Eastleach Turville. The 14th-c. N transept has three beautiful Decorated windows, with some delightful stone carving. Both churches have clear glass in the windows, which makes them attractively light. (See also *Walk 2*, p.19.)

Ebrington
C1
Village off B4035, 2m NE of Chipping Campden

Thatched roofs, instead of stone slates, are a feature of this village at the N edge of the Cotswolds. *St Eadburga's Church* has a Norman nave and doorways and an over-restored 13th-c. chancel. It contains a painted stone monument to Sir John Fortescue (d. 1484), represented rather larger than life and wearing the robes of the Lord Chief Justice, which office he held while lord of the manor at Ebrington. There is also a classical marble monument with busts of Sir John Keyt (d. 1662) and his wife. The pulpit and lectern are both 17th-c.

Elkstone
B3
Village off A417, 7m NW of Cirencester

Referred to in the Domesday Book as The Stone of Ealac, Elkstone is a lonely upland village, with perhaps the most perfect Norman church in the Cotswolds, **St John's**. It has an exquisite stone-vaulted chancel with a tiny E window, and a magnificently decorated chancel arch. The whole inside of the church is rich with Norman carvings: curious animals and birds, signs of the Zodiac and grotesque masks. The S doorway is ornamented with beakheads, while the tympanum shows Christ in Majesty. The fine W tower is a Perpendicular addition. A very unusual feature of the church is a large dovecote with 40 nesting places above the chancel, built after the original tower was destroyed. It is reached by a little spiral staircase near the pulpit. The *Priest's House* is late 15th- or early 16th-c., while the *Rectory* is an elegant, square Georgian house.

Fairford C4
Small town on A417, 9m E of Cirencester.
EC Sat.

Situated on the River Coln, this ancient market town is known amongst anglers for its trout fishing, but its principal claim to fame is its fine wool church, **St Mary's**, with its 28 magnificent stained glass windows.

Except for the base of the early 15th-c. tower, the church was completely re-built in the late Perpendicular style by John Tame, a rich wool merchant, and finished by his son, Sir Edmund Tame. The *windows* were made by the work-shop of Barnard Flower, Henry VII's Master Glass Painter, who was also responsible for the windows of Westminster Abbey's Lady Chapel and of King's College Chapel, Cambridge. John Tame's idea was to present the entire story of the Bible, beginning with Adam and Eve outside the Lady Chapel and ending with the Last Judgement in the great W window, with its red devils wreaking torments on the lost souls. The W windows had to be restored after they were blown in during the great gale of 1703, but all retain much of the original 15th-c. glass.

Other notable features of the church include the intricately carved – and very rare – oak screens round the chancel; the four hatted figures with swords at the corners of the tower; the stone angels supporting the roof trusses; and the exquisitely carved misericords on the choir stalls: a dog stealing food from a cooking pot, a woman pulling off a man's shoe, a fox carrying a dead duck in its mouth, a woman dragging a man by his hair – all the work of a gifted and humorous craftsman.

Set below a carved wooden arch between choir and Lady Chapel is John Tame's Purbeck marble tomb-chest, on which are brasses of him and his wife. In the *Lady Chapel*, on the wall, are brasses to Sir Edmund Tame and his two wives; also, a large tomb-chest with recumbent effigies of Roger Lygon and his wife Katharine, widow of Sir Edmund Tame II. The church also contains tablets to John Keble and his father. John Keble was born in Keble

House in the London Road in 1792 and lived here until 1835, after the publication of *The Christian Year*.

Next to the church is an 18th-c. *Free-School*, with a tablet on the wall facing the churchyard to Richard Green, master in 1767. From here the High Street leads to *Market Place*, Fairford's attractive main square. *The Bull Inn*, a restored 17th-c. building, takes up almost the whole of one side. Beyond the church are the gates of *Fairford Park*; the mansion was demolished in the 1950s and a school now stands on the site. W of the town is the site of an Anglo-Saxon *cemetery*, where 130 graves were uncovered last century.

Farmington C3
Village off A40, 1½m NE of Northleach

A quiet, peaceful place, right away from main roads, with many fine trees, a sloping green bordered by stone cottages, and good open views. The 1898 octagonal *Pumphouse* on the green originally had a thatched roof; the actual tiled roof was presented in 1935 by the inhabitants of Farmington, Connecticut, to commemorate the founding of their Farmington 300 years earlier. The church and lodge are away from the green, amidst large trees. *St Peter's Church* has a fine Norman S doorway with chevroned arch, and a Norman chancel arch with similar mouldings. The porch is 14th-c. and the tower late Perpendicular. *Farmington Lodge* is a rather grand Georgian mansion, with four giant Doric columns on the entrance front and 18th-c. stables and circular dovecote opposite. The *Rectory* is of the same period.

½m W of the village is *Norbury Camp*, an ancient British fort, and just S of that, on the other side of the country road, is a particularly fine 150ft-long *long barrow*.

Frocester A4
Village off A419, 5m SW of Stroud

Situated in the plains below the Edge, Frocester has possibly the largest **Tithe Barn** in England – 186ft long by 30ft wide. Built before 1306, it is one of the oldest and best preserved in the country. If Frocester is approached from the S, coming down Frocester Hill with its magnificent views over the Severn Vale, the barn can be seen on the right, and, next to it, *Frocester Court*, an attractive 15th-16th-c. house with a delightful half-timbered gateway. Queen Elizabeth I is reputed to have stayed here. Ask at the house for permission to look at the barn – it is if anything even more impressive inside than out and, happily, still used as a farm building.

The small village is centred upon a crossroads, overlooked by the pleasant-looking *Royal Gloucester Hussar*, a white-painted inn. *St Andrew's Church* is mainly 19th-c., the older one – *St Peter's* – having been demolished, except for its Victorian tower, in 1952.

Great Barrington see *Barringtons*

Great Rissington see *Rissingtons*

Great Witcombe   B3
Village off A417, 5½m S of Cheltenham
Set in a park-like bowl beneath the scarp edge at Birdlip Hill, with the beautiful Witcombe Wood to the SE, the village consists of a few scattered cottages, farms and *St Mary's Church* – Norman in origin with an 18th-c. tower and porch.

½m SW of the village, **Witcombe Roman Villa** is reached by a long single-track road signposted from the foot of Birdlip Hill. The excavated walls of the villa show the extent of what must have been a large and most beautifully sited building. Unfortunately the huts which have been built over the mosaics and bath-houses are never open, and there are no plans on the site to help the visitor appreciate what the original building would have been like.

Guiting Power   C2
Village off A436, 8m W of Stow-on-the-Wold
A typical Cotswold village consisting of a jumble of little stone cottages built round a green on the westward slope of the Windrush valley. The Norman *St Michael's Church* has been added to at various stages: the chancel in the latter part of the 12th c., the tower in the 15th

c., and the transepts in the 19th c., but it has very fine Norman doorways, particularly the S. The 1903 restoration was very carefully done: by the Norman priest's door and small window in the chancel is a plaque stating: 'At the restoration of 1903 these were not disturbed.' The village also contains a 16th-c. *Manor House*, a *Bakery* built *c.* 1600, and a 17th-c. mill, known as *The Dyers*, on a site mentioned in the Domesday Book, with the wheel still in place. *Guiting Grange*, built in 1848, is set in an attractive deer park. For several years Guiting Power has won the best-kept village award.

3m to the NE is the **Cotswold Farm Park** at Bemborough Farm. To reach it, start off following directions for Temple Guiting, then turn right at Kineton. Bemborough Farm will then appear on the right about 1m along the road. The Cotswold Farm Park is a unique survival centre for rare breeds of farm animals. The traditional 'Cotswold Lions' that brought wealth to so much of the Cotswolds, and many more species of sheep, cows, pigs and horses, including some delightful Iron Age pigs, can be seen. High on the hills, 900ft above sea level, this is an exhilarating and fascinating place to visit, with wide grassy walks between the large, unobtrusively fenced enclosures where the animals are kept. (See also *Walk 5*, p.19).

Hailes Abbey (NT)   C2
Ancient site off A46, 2m NE of Winchcombe
The abbey was founded by Richard, Earl of Cornwall (younger brother of Henry III), in 1245, for the white monks of Citeaux (Cistercians), in thanksgiving for his escape from imminent shipwreck. The dedication took place six years later, in the presence of the king and queen. In 1270 a phial of Christ's blood was presented to the Abbey by Edmund, Richard's second son, and a magnificent shrine, backed by five radiating chapels, was built behind the high altar of the 340ft-long church to house the precious relic. Hailes thus became one of England's greatest pilgrim centres: Chaucer has a pardoner swear 'by the blode of Crist

that is in Hayles'. In its heyday the great abbey owned 13,000 acres of land, but at its dissolution on Christmas Eve 1539 only the abbot and 20 monks remained. The Holy Blood had already been confiscated and discredited: it was declared to be 'an unctuous gum, coloured', and destroyed. The Abbey was then stripped of its plate and ornaments, and the lead from its roof; the buildings were later used as a stone quarry.

The ruin is now owned by the National Trust. Only parts of the cloister arches and walling remain above ground, but recent excavations have exposed the foundations. With its smooth green lawns, fine trees, and beautiful, tranquil setting, the place retains a strong atmosphere. The **Museum** is excellent, with exhibits detailing the history of the Abbey, some beautifully carved stone bosses and a collection of floor tiles.

Opposite the Abbey is **Hailes Church**, built in 1130, over 100 years before the abbey which later owned it, but much altered in the 14th c. Outside, its most notable feature is the tiny half-timbered tower, but inside it has many treasures: panels of medieval stained glass depicting nine Apostles, which were removed from the Abbey at the Dissolution; an unspoilt 15th-c. rood screen and 17th-c. furnishings; 300 13th-c. heraldic tiles from the Abbey set into the stone-flagged floor; a 13th-c. font; and extensive remains of medieval wall paintings – the three dogs hunting a crouching hare are particularly delightful.

Hampnett
C3
Village off A429, 1m NW of Northleach

An unspoilt village, with cottages thinly scattered round the large, hummocky green. A little spring – the infant Leach – gushes out of a stone trough at the upper end, then makes its way across the green and past a delightful row of cottages, one terrace gabled, one not. *St George's Church*, just beyond the lower end of the green, is surrounded by large barns. It is late Norman, with 15th-c. additions. It has a stone-vaulted

sanctuary and a little choir, with carved capitals representing doves drinking from a bowl, neck to neck. The chancel walls were decorated by Clayton and Bell and the Rev W. Wiggin *c.* 1871. With good open views from the green, Hampnett is a perfect place to walk about on a sunny day.

Harnhill
C4
Village off A419 or A417, 3½m SE of Cirencester

Although Harnhill itself is not particularly notable, its medieval church, *St Michael's*, is delightful, its little tower hung with stone slates like the roof. The Norman tympanum over the mutilated S doorway, showing St Michael fighting the dragon, should not be missed. There are also pieces of medieval glass in the E window. The *Manor House*, to the E of the church, 16th-c. with an 18th-c. front, is a most attractive building. The *Old Rectory*, to the W, is 17th-c. altered in the Gothic style *c.* 1810.

Hatherop
C3
Village off A417, 3m N of Fairford

With Williamstrip Park to the N and Hatherop Castle to the S, Hatherop is a 19th-c. estate village largely surrounded by parkland. *Williamstrip Park*, the home of Lord St Aldwyn, is a square late 17th-c. classical stone house, set at the top of a hill overlooking its superb park. *Hatherop Castle*, a large battlemented Elizabethan and Jacobean manor house, remodelled in 1850-6 and now a girls' school, has an equally spectacular setting, with the River Coln making a great loop in the valley below.

St Nicholas' Church, situated close to the house, is approached by a footpath from the village. It was completely remodelled at the same time as Hatherop Castle, and is rather dull inside, but do not fail to see Raffaelle Monti's exquisitely carved effigy of Barbara, Lady de Maulay, in the S mortuary chapel: she lies, in white marble, almost as if she were asleep, a mourning angel on either side. The finely carved stone frieze round the chapel has castles, leaves, flowers and 'Bs' for Barbara.

Hidcote Manor (NT) C1

Gardens off B4081, 3½m NE of Chipping Campden

These famous gardens, now owned by the National Trust, were created by the American, Laurence Johnston, who bought the 17th-c. *Manor House* in 1907. Here, countless small gardens lead one into another, each separated from the next by high, secluding hedges of yew, holly, box and beech. There is also a delightful wooded dell, which shelters many rare plants. No grand sweep of lawn from the house, no stately design for this garden: only at the very edge of the gardens will a grassy path suddenly lead to a wrought-iron gate and the spreading Cotswold hills beyond. Much original botanical work has been done here, and many plants now bear the name 'Hidcote'.

Just opposite are the lovely gardens of *Kiftsgate Court*, and ¾m to the S is *Hidcote House*, a very fine, L-shaped house built in 1663.

Honington Hall D1

Warwickshire. Historic house off A34, 2m NE of Shipston-on-Stour

Built in 1682 for Sir Henry Parker, a rich London merchant, on the site of an earlier house, of which only the stables and dovecote survive, this is a perfect example of late 17th-c. architecture. The interior was remodelled *c.* 1740-50 by Joseph Townsend, who bought the house from the Parkers. The splendid stucco ceilings and mythological stucco reliefs on the walls date from this period. Most elaborate is the plaster-work in the *Entrance Hall* and *Stairway*, and in the great octagonal *Saloon*, with its fine domed ceiling.

The house was originally linked to the small *All Saints' Church* nearby. This is of the same date as the house, and contains some good monuments, including a Baroque one to Sir Henry Parker and his son Hugh, shown standing side by side, and a Rococo one to Joseph Townsend (d. 1763). The church has a 13th-c. tower but is otherwise classical, *c.* 1680. The royal arms of the House of Stuart can be seen above the chancel arch.

Icomb D2

Village off A424, 3m SE of Stow-on-the-Wold

Icomb is a charming little village with several 17th- and 18th-c. cottages. The small Early English *St Mary's Church* has an interesting tower, built *c.* 1600, with a gabled saddleback roof and domestic Tudor windows. The chancel is Early English, but the inside is slightly disappointing, with the exception of the chantry chapel of Sir John Blaket (died 1431). A recumbent effigy of a knight in armour rests under a canopy on a tomb-chest with carved figures. *Icomb Place* was rebuilt *c.* 1420, probably by Sir John Blaket. The S side is entirely taken up by the great hall, which has an open timber roof.

Kelmscot D4

Village off B4449, 3m E of Lechlade

The village is best known for *Kelmscott Manor*, summer home of the poet and designer William Morris from 1871-96. The gabled 16th- and 17th-c. house is attractively sited among fields and willows on the N bank of the Thames and contains a fine collection of the work of Morris and fellow members of the Arts and Crafts movement. The house, owned by the Society of Antiquaries, is open for only one day a month in the summer.

The village, whose name was used by Morris for his private printing press, has a number of handsome 17th-c. stone farmhouses, and the *Morris Cottages* (1902) built by Philip Webb. Morris's grave in the churchyard of the 12th-c. *St George's Church* has a headstone carved by Webb. The church has some medieval paintings and stained glass.

Kempsford C4

Village off A417, 3m S of Fairford

A royal residence in Saxon days and, in the Middle Ages, the site of a castle which was the seat of the Earls of Lancaster, Kempsford today is a straggling village with 17th- and 18th-c. buildings and an interesting church, **St Mary the Virgin**. The nave is Norman, *c.* 1120 (the oak roof was added in 1450); the Decorated chancel was added by Henry

Plantagenet, Earl of Lancaster, *c.* 1340, while the fine tower, 1390-99, was added by John of Gaunt in memory of his wife, Lady Blanche of Plantagenet, mother of Henry IV and patroness of Chaucer. The ornate circular vault is painted with heraldic shields. Monuments include the recumbent effigy of a tonsured priest, *c.* 1450, on top of a panelled tomb-chest.

The adjacent large *Manor Farm* was rebuilt in 1846 by Sir Gilbert East on the site of the former castle but the farm's *Barn* goes back to the 17th c., as does the *vicarage.*

Kiftsgate Court
C1
Gardens off B4081, 3½m N of Chipping Campden

Just opposite the entrance to *Hidcote Manor*, the gardens of Kiftsgate Court are very different. They have been arranged on a hillside so steep one would have thought gardening impossible. Flowering shrubs and delicate woodland plants edge the terraced paths that ultimately lead to a smooth green lawn and a swimming pool. With massed trees and shrubs curving round behind, and green fields and grazing cows ahead, this is an idyllic spot. The gardens round the house, with their fine views over the valley below, are famous for their old-fashioned roses.

Kingscote
A4
Village off A4135, 4m SW of Nailsworth

Judging from the monuments in the church and churchyard, this village was very much dominated by the Kingscote family. They owned the manor from the 12th c., only selling *Kingscote Grange*, a late Georgian house, in 1956. Another home, Kingscote Park, was demolished in 1851 – the same year that the 13th-c. church, *St John's*, was heavily restored. In the church, the chancel walls are covered with Kingscote memorials. (Note particularly the moving monument to the infant Henry Kingscote, the life-like child in his cold marble bed.) In the porch is a tablet commemorating the marriage in 1788 of Catherine Kingscote to Edward Jenner, pioneer of vaccination.

King's Stanley
A4
Village off A419, 3m SW of Stroud

The village is almost completely overwhelmed by modern development, but, when driving through, look out for *Stanley Mill*. Built *c.* 1812, it is the largest and grandest Georgian cloth mill in the Stroud valley. Five storeys high, it was the first fireproof building in England, built entirely of brick, stone and iron. The original plant continued to run until 1954.

Lechlade
D4
Small town on A417 and A361, 13m E of Cirencester

As its main Market Place is near the junction of two main roads, Lechlade suffers from constant traffic; nevertheless, it is a pleasant little town with some interesting domestic architecture lining its streets – particularly *Burford Street* – and a rare wholly Perpendicular church, **St Lawrence's**, re-dedicated in the early 16th c., when Catherine of Aragon held the manor. This 'wool' church has a spacious, light interior, with a fine chancel roof decorated with carved bosses. Monuments include a brass to a wool merchant, John Townsend (d. 1458), and his wife in the N aisle. The *N porch*, an early 16th-c. addition – possibly from Lechlade's earlier Priory – has a Tudor rose. It opens onto what is now called *Shelley's Walk*, where there is a wall plaque quoting from his poem, written in 1815, 'A Summer Evening Churchyard, Lechlade':

Here could I hope
That death did hide from human sight
Sweet secrets

The square, early 18th-c. *Downington House* is under 1m to the W, while the same distance SW, at the junction of the rivers Thames and Coln – and the former Severn-Thames Canal – stands the late 18th-c. *Round House*, a canal maintenance men's place, with cottage and stone bridge. There are two other bridges: the 17th-c. *Halfpenny Bridge*, by the boatyard, and the rebuilt successor of a very early Thames bridge, *St John's Bridge*, where yet another river, the Leach, helps to swell the Thames which, from Lechlade downstream, becomes a navigable river. 3m W of Lechlade off the B4449 is Kelmscott Manor, home of William Morris, in the village of *Kelmscot. (See also *Walk 3*, p.19.)

Leckhampton   B3
Village off A46 and B4070, 1m S of Cheltenham

Leckhampton is virtually a suburb of Cheltenham. *St Peter's Church* is largely 14th-c., with a central tower and vaulted chancel. The fine effigies of the fierce-looking Sir John Giffard (d. 1327) and his wife, and the late 16th-c. brass to Elizabeth Norwood, shown with her husband and eleven children – both in the S aisle – should not be missed. In the churchyard is a granite cross recording the death of Edward Wilson, an Antarctic explorer, who lived at *The Crippetts* nearby. *Leckhampton Court*, where the Giffards lived for centuries, is also partly 14th c., and retains its old banqueting hall.

¾m to the S, on the E side of the B4070, is *Leckhampton Hill*, the western part of Charlton Kings Common, almost 1000ft high. On the summit are the remains of a British *hill fort*, and just to the W is the *Devil's Chimney*, a remnant of the extensive quarries that existed here until the early part of this century. It was from the pale creamy stone of Leckhampton Hill that Cheltenham was built. This is a marvellous place for walking, with magnificent views. Leckhampton Hill Walk is a short, well marked walk. (See also *Walk 6*, p.20.)

Leonard Stanley   A4
Village off A419, 4m SW of Stroud

At first sight this village seems little more than an undistinguished suburb of Stroud, but on turning off the main road to the church an attractive village green, with a row of stone cottages facing the church, is reached.

The village takes its name from the Priory of St Leonard founded by Roger Berkeley between 1121-29, and the original priory church, **St Swithin's** is virtually intact. It is exceptionally fine and quite unlike the rather small, dark churches usually associated with the Normans. Inside, it is light and spacious, with a wide aisleless nave and a large open area under the massive central tower. All the windows have clear glass. Only the N porch, the 14th-c. wagon roof and some of the windows are later additions. There are some fascinating stone carvings. Of particular interest are the 'picture' capitals in the chancel, showing Mary Magdalene washing Jesus's feet and the Birth of Our Lord; the reset tympanum over the aumbry on the S of the chancel showing Adam and Eve as animals; and the crocodile-like beasts on the corbels of the N porch.

The priory was immediately to the S of the church. The remaining buildings include an 11th-c. *Church*, assumed to have been the parish church before the foundation of the priory, and subsequently used as a farm building, and a fine *Tithe Barn*.

Little Barrington see *Barringtons*

Little Rissington see *Rissingtons*

Longborough   C2
Village off A424, 3m N of Stow-on-the-Wold

On a hillside overlooking the Evenlode Valley, this attractive village has several good 17th-c. farmhouses and cottages and an inn, *The Coach and Horses* with ales from the local *Donnington Brewery. St James's Church* has Norman remains, including the N and S doorways, but its finest feature is the beautiful early 14th-c. *S transept* with its large Decorated window. Here lies a 14th-c. effigy of a knight in armour, for whom the transept was probably built, and the splendid black and white marble tomb of Sir William Leigh (d. 1631) and his wife, with their three infant children. The N transept, or *Sezincote Chapel*, was added by Sir Charles Cockerell of Sezincote in 1822-3, and contains his tomb. The only entrance is by an outside doorway leading to the family pew. The church also contains a fine 14th-c. font.

Lower Guiting see *Guiting Power*

Lower Slaughter see *Slaughters*

Lower Swell see *Swells*

Mickleton   C1
Village on A46, 3m N of Chipping Campden

Situated just below the Cotswold Edge, with the outlying Meon Hill to the NE, Mickleton is usually considered the northernmost Cotswold village. This border position is reflected in the mixture of timber-framed, thatched cottages and traditional Cotswold stone. The medieval *St Lawrence's Church* has a 17th-c. two-storey porch, a 12th-c. rood cross over the N aisle chapel altar and some good 18th-c. tablets. *Medford House*, built c. 1694, is a perfect example of the transition from Tudor to Queen Anne classical style. The little memorial *fountain* in front of *The Three Ways Hotel* was designed by William Burges in 1875.

The lovely gardens of *Hidcote Manor* and *Kiftsgate Court* are just over 1m to the SE.

Middle Duntisbourne see *Duntisbourne*

Minchinhampton   B4
Small town off A419, 4m SE of Stroud. EC Thur

Once a busy cloth-making centre, Minchinhampton is now a peaceful little town, centred round an attractive *Market Square*. The most conspicuous building in the square is the **Market House**, built in 1698 and supported by stone and wooden columns, but there are many other good stone houses in the square, including the 18th-c. *Crown Hotel*.

Holy Trinity Church, with its rather ugly truncated spire, faces on to the square; the path through the churchyard is lined with a mass of colourful rockery flowers. Unfortunately, the nave, chancel and aisles were very unattractively rebuilt in 1842, with village hall-like roofs to the aisles and the wall monuments reset round the clerestory windows. There is also an ugly modern porch. However, the 14th-c. S transept

is exceptionally beautiful, possibly built by the John of Ansley who, with his wife Lucy, lies in effigy beneath the great Decorated S window. The N transept and tower are also 14th-c., but the spire was taken down to its present height in 1563. All the older brasses in the church have been lifted and reset on stone slabs by the W door, but there is a wall brass to James Bradley, Astronomer Royal in 1762, on the wall of the S transept; he is buried in the churchyard. The painted decorations on the chancel roof were done in 1931 by F.C. Eden.

To the N and W of the town is **Minchinhampton Common** (NT). These 600 acres of common land were given to the town by Dame Alice Hampton during the reign of Henry VIII. *The Bulwarks*, 1m W of the church, are Iron Age defensive works consisting of a massive rampart and ditch. They were built at or just before the Roman Conquest in AD 43, and defend about 600 acres of land, including the area of *Amberley Camp*, an Iron Age hill fort. This part of the common is now largely a golf course. In the middle of the common, a signpost where six roads meet marks the place where highwaymen caught on the common were buried. Strewn with buttercups, and with cows and horses grazing, the whole common is a good place for walking, and *The Halfway House* inn is a nice place for a drink and snack.

1m SE of Minchinhampton is *Gatcombe Park*. Built in 1771-4, it was bought in 1814 by David Ricardo, the political economist, and later owned by Lord (R.A.) Butler. It is now the home of Princess Anne and Mark Phillips.

Miserden   B3
Village off B4070, 7½m NE of Stroud

Miserden's *St Andrew's Church* is late Saxon in origin, but it was greatly spoilt by 19th-c. restorers. The heads of the N and S doorways are still visibly Saxon, however. Inside, the church has some outstanding 17th-c. tombs. The finest is that of Sir William Sandys (died 1640) and his wife Margaret Culpeper, carved

76

in alabaster with their children round the tomb-chest. There is also a delightful tablet dated 1625 in the chancel, with kneeling effigies in a Renaissance setting, and a good 19th-c. wall monument with a weeping angel.

Misarden Park, superbly set at the top of the steep, wooded valley of the Frome, dates from *c.* 1616, with a new wing designed by Sir Edwin Lutyens in 1920-1. The *Gardens* are open two days a week in the summer.

Moreton-in-Marsh   D2
Small town on A429/A44, 4½m N of Stow-on-the-Wold. Event: Moreton-in-Marsh Show (1st Sat in Sep). EC Wed. MD Tue. Inf: Tel (0608) 50881

The exceptionally broad, tree-lined **High Street** along which this pleasant little market town is mainly built is part of the Fosse Way. Most of the houses were built in the 18th and 19th c., when the town was a local linen-weaving centre and an important stopping-place for coaches – reflected in the number of old inns. It is a local tradition that Charles I stayed a night at *The White Hart Hotel* in 1644. The opening of the railway station in 1843 encouraged the further growth of the town.

The handsome *Market Hall* in the centre of the High Street was built in 1887 by Sir Ernest George in Tudor style, while the 13th-c. *St David's Church* was almost completely rebuilt, in 13th- and 14th-c. styles, in 1842. Probably the oldest building in the town is the 16th-c. *Curfew Tower* on the corner of Oxford Street, with a bell that was rung daily until 1860. There is an excellent street market every Tuesday, and the Moreton-in-Marsh Show, a big agricultural and horse show, is held in September.

1½m E of the town on the A44, by the junction with the Great Wolford road, is the *Four Shires Stone*, an 18th-c. monument with Gloucestershire, Worcestershire, Warwickshire and Oxfordshire inscribed on the appropriate faces.

3m N, off the A429 at Aston Magna is the *Bygones Museum*, a small collection of farm and domestic equipment and a brass-rubbing centre.

Nailsworth   A4
Small town on A46, 4½m S of Stroud. EC Thur

An ancient wool town and later an important cloth-making centre, built on the steep hillsides of the valley of the Avon stream. Most of the important mills are on the Stroud road, including *Egypt Mills* and *Dunkirk Mills*, the largest mill building in the district, of which the oldest part is 18th-19th-c. The Anglican *St George's Church* was built as recently as 1900, but the *Friends' Meeting House* is one of the oldest in the country, built in 1689. Overlooking a delightful little cobbled courtyard, it retains its original furnishings. There are several other Non-Conformist chapels in the town.

Naunton   C2
Village off A436, 5m SW of Stow-on-the-Wold

This long, narrow village spreads about 1m along the Windrush valley, just below the main Stow-Cheltenham road. *St Andrew's Church* stands at the W end of the village, on a little knoll. It was largely rebuilt in the 16th c., but the tower, with its pinnacles and gargoyles, is 15th-c. Its great treasure is the carved stone pulpit, dated *c.* 1400; it also has a 15th-c. carved font and a 17th-c. brass in the N aisle. The tablets to Dr William Oldys, 'barbarously murthered by ye Rebells in ye yeare 1645', and his son Ambrose, who died in 1710 with 'better fortune' should not be missed. Overlooking the stream, not far from the 17th-c. *Manor House*, is a large gabled dovecot, built *c.* 1600, with 1000 nesting places. Almost the last building at the E end of the village is the 17th-c. *Naunton Mill*; the wooden machinery was only renewed in 1964 when it was converted into a house.

North Cerney   C3
Village on A435, 4m N of Cirencester

North Cerney is a pleasant village, but the best things about it are undoubtedly the pub and the church. *The Bathurst Arms*, a long, low, pink-washed building, has a delightful garden by the Churn and excellent food, while **All Saints' Church**, on the opposite side of the river, is of exceptional interest.

Among its treasures are a richly ornamented Norman S doorway; sculptured stone corbels on the nave roof; a Georgian gallery; an exceptionally fine pulpit of *c.* 1480, the bowl cut from a single piece of stone and decorated with lilies; 15th-c. glass in the transept windows; three 15th-c. painted statues, of the Virgin and two bishops, in the reredos in the S transept; and a marble monument with a mourning figure dated 1783. The church owes its present beautiful state to the benefactions of the late William Iveson Croome, whose friend F.C. Eden designed the rood loft and the screen to the Lady Chapel, amongst other things. The *Rectory* opposite is late 17th c.

Northleach

C3

Village on A40, 9m NW of Burford

An important centre for the wool trade in the Middle Ages, and a busy staging post on the main coaching road from London to Gloucester in the late 18th and early 19th c., Northleach today is a peaceful little place, almost undisturbed by the tourists who pass through it on the A40. The triangular *Market Place*, with its cross, post office and row of shops, offers an attractive layby: the tower of the church rising in the background a further point of interest.

Approaching the church of **St Peter and St Paul** the visitor should not be surprised to find sheep grazing amidst the gravestones. The church, rebuilt in the 15th c., is a model of the Perpendicular style. One of its glories is the *S porch*, with crocketed pinnacles, buttresses and medieval images on the outside and fine vaulting inside (the carved corbels here are worth noting – particularly that of a cat fiddling to three rats).

Inside the church one can see the work endowed by the wool merchant John Fortey, who rebuilt the nave and added the great clerestory, with its magnificent nine-light window over the chancel arch, to make the church more 'lightsome and splendid'. There is much to look at in the church – the 15th-c. pulpit, the 14th-c. carved font,

the roof corbels in the Lady Chapel showing Henry VII and Elizabeth of York – but its greatest treasures are the wool merchants' brasses. In the middle of the N aisle there is a 5ft brass of John Fortey (d. 1459), his feet resting on a woolpack, and at the end, up the steps, another to his father Thomas, his wife Agnes, her first husband William Scors (a tailor – hence the scissors), and the children of both marriages. The brass of William Midwinter (d. 1501) and his wife shows both with their feet resting on sheep. The emblems of the wool trade that made these men rich are everywhere evident in the church.

To the E of Market Place lies another triangular space, *The Green*, now used as a car park. Here is the half-timbered *Tudor House*, where John Fortey is supposed to have lived. The stone corbels on either side of the carriage entrance show a device which is said to have been his badge. Up the lane and round the corner, passing a splendid *Tithe Barn*, a short walk leads past a redundant mill, converted into a house, to *Mill End*, with its mill pond on the River Leach.

At the crossroads to the W of the village is the **Cotswold Countryside Collection**, a museum of rural life and agricultural history. The collection is superbly arranged in Northleach's former 'model' prison opened in 1792. The buildings comprise the keeper's house in the centre with a block on either side: on the left the old infirmary, later a police station; on the right the women's cell block. The main five-sided cell block enclosing the compound was demolished in the '30s.

Notgrove

C3

Village off B4068, 4m N of Northleach

A high, rather lonely village, with most of the cottages built round a large, rough green. The church and manor house are a little way beyond, approached by an impressive tree-lined drive and beautifully situated overlooking the valley of a little stream. *St Bartholomew's Church* is basically Norman, but much restored in the 19th c. In the chancel are three late 16th- early 17th-c.

effigies of members of the Whittington family – descendants of Dick Whittington – who lived at the manor house, and in the N transept there are two very worn late 14th-c. effigies of priests, which lay outside in the churchyard for many centuries. Over the remains of the reredos hangs a fine tapestry of the village, completed in 1954. Finally, on the outside of the E wall is a small, much weathered Saxon stone crucifix. The *Manor House* is 17th-c. in origin but largely rebuilt.

1m to the NW, just S of the A436, are the excavated remains of a *long barrow*. The mound has almost gone, so the burial chambers can be seen. Human skeletons and Neolithic pottery were found here in 1934-5; they are now in the Cheltenham Museum.

Oddington   D2
Village off A436, 2½m E of Stow-on-the-Wold

An interesting village with several good houses. *Oddington House* was built *c.* 1600; it was enlarged in the early 19th c. and has a beautiful Regency interior (not open to the public). The *Old Rectory*, next door, is 17th-c., altered in the 19th. There is a 'new' Victorian church in the village: the old church, *St Nicholas*, is isolated to the SE, the site of an earlier abandoned village.

The church is well worth a visit. 12th-c. in origin, it was enlarged in the 13th c. by the addition of a new nave and chancel on the N side: the original nave and chancel are the present S aisle and chapel. The tower is also 13th-c., with a 15th-c. top stage. On the N wall of the nave is a large 14th-c. Doom wall painting, recently restored. The church also has a good carved Jacobean pulpit and a 15th-c. carved font. In the churchyard lies the recumbent effigy of Margaret Parsons (d. *c.* 1695).

Owlpen   A4
Hamlet off B4066, 3m E of Dursley

Situated in a peaceful little valley below a wooded hill, and sheltered from the road by huge yews, **Owlpen Manor** has a perfect setting. It is not a large house, but full of interest, and medieval in ori-

gin. The Hall and Great Chamber above were added *c.* 1540; the W wing, with its embattled bay window, is dated 1616, and the E wing was altered and sash windows added at the beginning of the 18th c. The house stood empty from *c.* 1850, when a new Victorian mansion was built higher up the hill; but Norman Jewson bought and restored it in 1926, and the new mansion was demolished in 1955. Inside, the house is charming, and little altered since the early 18th c. The complete set of late 17th-c. painted cloth wall hangings in the *Great Chamber* is said to be unique. The house can only be visited by written appointment, but it is worth stopping just to look at the outside.

It is also well worth having a look at the **Church of the Holy Cross** behind the house. It is Victorian, and decorated with late Pre-Raphaelite mosaics, tiles and paintings. The chancel ceiling is painted with sun and stars, while the walls are covered by brilliant tiles and mosaics; angels and lilies, in tiles and mosaics, adorn the baptistery; the organ pipes are painted grey and white with orange crowns and tongues of fire; the floor is tiled in red, yellow and black. The church contains eight wall brasses to members of the Daunt family, dating from 1542 to 1803: John Daunt married Marjery Ollepen in 1464.

Ozleworth   A4
Hamlet off A4135, 2½m E of Wotton-under-Edge

A long way from anywhere, and approached by the narrowest of lanes, muddy and half-flooded after heavy rain, Ozleworth is perhaps only for the true church enthusiast. To reach *St Nicholas' Church*, drive through the grounds of Ozleworth Park and past the house. The Norman church has a rare hexagonal central tower; this is the oldest part of the church, and may once have been the nave. The W tower arch leading on to the nave, and the S doorway with its ornate stiff-leaf sprays, are fine Early English work, as is the font. The church is set in a circular churchyard which is, sadly, completely overgrown. *Ozleworth Park* itself is a fine Georgian house, with a large Regency addition on the N, beautifully set at the head of its park.

Painswick   A3/B3
Small town on A46, 3m N of Stroud. Events: Guild of Glos. Craftsmen Exhibition & Market (1st 3 weeks in Aug); Clipping Ceremony (Sat nearest Sep 19). EC Sat. Inf: Tel (0452) 812569

On a spur on the W edge of the Cotswolds, Painswick is an attractive unspoilt town with narrow streets and grey stone buildings, some medieval and many dating from the 17th and 18th c., when Painswick was an important centre for the cloth industry.

St Mary's Church is famous for the unequalled collection of 17th and 18th c. table-tombs and the clipped yews – many of them 200 years old – in the churchyard. There are said to be 99 of these trees, though no-one has been able to count them exactly. The ceremony of 'clipping', held each September, when the parishioners join hands to encircle their church, has nothing to do with clipping the yews, however. 'Clipping' here comes from the Anglo-Saxon word for 'embracing' – *clippen*. The iron stocks at the churchyard gate are thought to be unique.

The church itself was mainly built in the 15th c., but the tall spire, which has twice been struck by lightning and rebuilt, dates from 1632. The church was badly damaged by fire in 1644, when 'grenadoes' (an early form of hand grenade) were thrown into it by Royalists attacking some of Cromwell's men who had taken refuge in the building.

The oldest part of the church is *St Peter's Chapel*, in the N aisle, which dates from 1377-78 and which contains tombs of the families who used it. Most impressive is the tomb of Dr John Seaman (d. 1623) and his wife, of the Court House, shown kneeling beneath a canopy supported by a column balanced on a pile of law books.

Opposite the lych gate of the church, on the other side of New Street, are two adjoining 17th-c. houses: *Hazelbury House* and *Packers*. Hazelbury House had its Palladian front added in the 18th-c. Further up is *The Falcon Hotel* (1711) and the 17th-c. *Post Office*, built at the same time as the street, the only half-timbered building in Painswick. At the crossroads another 15th-c. building, *New Hall*, is on the right: this was a clothmaker's hall.

To the right, down Bisley Street, are even earlier buildings. First on the left are the 14th-c. *Wickstone* and *Little Fleece*. Now National Trust property, these buildings once formed *The Fleece Inn* (note the arch of the filled-in carriage entrance over the front window of *Wickstone*). *The Chur*, adjacent, is also 14th-c. and has an arched door for the use of donkeys carrying fleeces.

At the foot of Bisley Street to the left is Vicarage Street, with more interesting and attractive houses. A short way down on the right is the 17th-c. *Yew Tree House*, built for the clothier Thomas Loveday, which has yew trees that were planted before those of the church. Further on, also on the right, is the charming *Dover House* (1720), also built for the Lovedays, and behind it the odd-looking *Friends' Meeting House* (1706) where the Quaker family used to worship.

(A footpath leads from here downhill to the Painswick Stream where an old mill, *Savory's Pin Mill*, can be seen. A cloth mill until the 19th c., this was later used for the manufacture of pins. Now disused, the mill is scheduled for conversion into housing: other mills further along the stream are also now private houses. A road, Tibbiwell, leads back uphill to St Mary's Street behind the church.)

For those not taking the footpath diversion, St Mary's Street is reached by returning along Vicarage Street to the church. The 18th-c. *Vicarage* was originally another Loveday house. By the rear gate of the church are the stocks of 1840, and off the top of Hale Lane is the **Court House** (1600).

Amongst the finest of the houses in the surrounding area is **Painswick House**, ½m N, built in the 1730s with lower wings added a century later. A pleasant walk can be made 1½m N of the town to *Painswick Beacon*, a splendid viewpoint and the site of an Iron Age *hill fort* and a golf-course.

Prinknash Abbey B3
Monastery off A46, 3m N of Painswick

In 1928 Prinknash was given to the Benedictine monks of Caldey Island. At first they used the early 14th-c. grange of the Abbey of Gloucester, but in 1939 they began to build a new abbey. Completed in 1972, and built entirely by the monks themselves, it is a magnificently sited modern structure. The crypt *Church of Our Lady and St Peter* at the back is impressive in its simplicity, with its windows of contemporary stained glass.

The Abbey is famous for its *Pottery*. The work of the monks, the pottery can be bought, along with other Abbey products, at the shop. The pottery, and the 9-acre *Bird Park*, with over 60 species of birds, are open to the public.

Quenington C3
Village off A417 and A433, 2m N of Fairford

Quenington is an attractive village built on a hill which slopes down to the River Coln. *St Swithin's Church* stands at the lower end of the village. It was drastically restored in 1882, but the superb Norman *doorways* remain untouched. The tympanum over the N doorway represents the Harrowing of Hell: Our Lord is shown piercing Satan, bound hand and foot, with a cross. The tympanum on the S doorway shows the Coronation of the Virgin, while the inner arch of the doorway itself is decorated with beak-heads and the heads of an ox and a horse. Near the church is *Quenington Court*, built on the site of the Preceptory of the Knights Hospitaller. The house itself is 19th-c., but the medieval gatehouse and a round dovecote survive.

Rendcomb B3/C3
Village on A435, 5½m N of Cirencester

Sir Edmund Tame of Fairford held the manor here at the beginning of the 16th c., and he rebuilt the church, after the completion of Fairford Church in 1517. As at Fairford, **St Peter's Church** re-

tains the carved wooden screens round the chancel (they are almost identical to those at Fairford, and could well be by the same carver); it also has some good Renaissance glass. The famous *Rendcomb font* was brought into the church at a later date, probably by the Guises, who bought the manor in the 17th c. It is pure Norman, with carvings of eleven Apostles in an arcade– the figure of Judas has been left uncarved. Amongst the other things of interest in this treasure-trove of a church are the angel corbels – especially two near the S doorway, which carry musical instruments; the door itself, which is the original one; the tombs of some Berkeleys and Guises, former lords of the manor, in the S chapel, behind a mid-18th-c. wrought-iron screen; and a fine Baroque tablet to Jane Berkeley in the chancel.

The grand Italianate mansion that is now *Rendcomb College* was built by Philip Charles Hardwick in 1863. He also built the grandiose stable block, which is in the village.

Rissingtons, Great and Little, Wyck (Wick) Rissington D3/D2
Villages off the A429 and A424, respectively 3m SE, 1½m E and 3m NE of Bourton-on-the-Water

At the bottom of **Great Rissington**'s steep village street stand the *Church of St John the Baptist*, the 17th-c. *Manor House* (enlarged in 1929) and the early 18th-c. *Rectory*. The church is cruciform with a broad central tower rising from four pointed arches of c. 1200. Apart from this it was largely rebuilt, in early 13th-c. style, in 1873. It is rather dull inside, but the Jacobean tablet with miniature figures in the S transept and the large appliqué picture of the village made by the Women's Institute in the N transept should not be missed. The village street, with its widely spaced houses, runs uphill from the church to a little green and *The Lamb Inn*, a good place for lunch.

Little Rissington lies to the N, less than 1½m by footpath but 2½m by road. This village is also built on a hill, with a steep, winding street. *St Peter's Church* is set apart from the village, on the other side of a small ravine, over-looking the Windrush valley and Bourton-on-the-Water. The village, too, must originally have stood here: a large house near the church, demolished in the 17th c., was presumably the old manor. Unfortunately, the church was largely rebuilt in rather unpleasant stone in the 19th c., but inside it has an impressive arcade of two 12th-c. arches separating nave from aisle.

Wyck Rissington is another 1m to the N. Again, it is further by road, but the steep descent to the village from Wyck Beacon offers lovely views. It is an attractive village, with houses set well back from the road; they are scattered along the edges of the green that skirts both sides of the village street. The exterior of *St Laurence's Church*, with its massive 13th-c. tower, is more attractive than the interior, which is very dark, so that one can hardly see the tiny figures on the 16th-c. carved wooden plaques in the chancel. The chancel also contains a small window with 14th-c. glass, and the organ that Gustav Holst played when he was organist here in 1892-3; it was his first professional engagement.

Rodborough Common A4
High ground off A46, 1m S of Stroud

Rodborough itself is now little more than a hilly suburb of Stroud, but Rodborough Common is a marvellous place for walking, with fine views in all directions. It is part of a tongue of high, flat land between the Golden Valley and the Nailsworth valley, and it runs into Minchinhampton Common to the S. To the W of the common is *The Bear Hotel*, which has been an inn continuously since the 17th c. *Rodborough Fort* is a castellated 18th-c. house rebuilt in 1870.

Rodmarton B4
Village off A433, 4½m NE of Tetbury

Perhaps the most interesting building in Rodmarton is **Rodmarton Manor**, built between 1906-26 by Ernest Barnsley for the Hon Claud Biddulph. The materials were taken entirely from the estate, and the work was done by the estate employees. The house is built partly round a circular grass courtyard, and furnished by Ernest Gimson, Ernest and Sidney Barnsley, and Peter Waals. The *Gardens* are open once a week in the summer.

St Peter's Church and most of the cottages in the village are built facing a small green. The church is 13th- and 14th-c. The nave walls have unfortunately been scraped of plaster, but there are several interesting monuments, including a 15th-c. brass of a lawyer in cap and gown in the chancel; a monument dated 1678 to 'John Barnard, the Eminent Bone-setter'; a marble tablet to Charles George dated 1807, with the figures of his afflicted wife and little child; and several monuments to the Lysons family. Samuel Lysons the antiquary lived at Rodmarton: members of his family were rectors here for 137 years. It was Lysons who discovered the **Woodchester Roman Pavement*. He also published *A Collection of Gloucestershire Antiquities* in 1804, with over 100 of his own drawings of buildings, statues, monuments and scenes of country life.

Rollright Stones D2
Ancient site off A34, 4m N of Chipping Norton

Located in the high, open country to the N of Chipping Norton, these dramatic standing stones merit a diversion from the A34 or A44 (Little Rollright).

A solitary stone to the N of the road is known as the *King Stone*. Opposite, on the other side of the road, is the main group, the *King's Men*, a Bronze Age stone circle consisting of a ring of stones about 100ft across. Originally there were 11, but many have been broken up. To the E is a group of four standing stones and a dislodged capstone known as the *Whispering Knights*: these would have been part of a Bronze Age burial mound.

Legend has it that a king, who was intent on conquering England, met a witch here. She turned him and his men into stones, and herself into an elder tree. Before turning herself into a tree, however, she went back and also turned into stone some knights who had lagged behind, apparently whispering together and plotting against the king.

The nearby hamlet of *Little Rollright* is worth visiting for *St Philip's Church*, a small Perpendicular building with two splendid 17th-c. monuments.

Salperton C3
Village off B4068, 6m NW of Northleach

Church and park are situated ¼m to the S of this tiny, isolated village. *Salperton Park* dates back to the 17th c., but was greatly enlarged in the 19th c. The public footpath to the church leads right across the front of the house, where a beautifully kept formal garden is incongruously surrounded by fields and pastures and rolling hills. The little *Church of All Saints* has a Norman chancel arch and a medieval wall painting of a skeleton holding a spear.

Sapperton B4
Village off A419, 5½m W of Cirencester

Situated high above the deep Frome Valley, its slopes clothed in beechwoods, Sapperton is an exceptionally attractive and interesting village. **St Kenelm's Church** is beautifully situated at the very top of the slope. Though medieval in origin, it was largely rebuilt in the reign of Queen Anne, with round-headed windows with clear glass and a great deal of fine wood carving – bench ends, panelling in the S transept, the front of the gallery and the cornice in the nave – all taken from Sapperton House when it was demolished by the first Lord Bathurst c. 1730. The church also contains some magnificent monuments: kneeling effigies of Sir Henry Poole (d. 1616) and his family, in a canopied Renaissance tomb; and the county historian, Sir Robert Atkyns (d. 1711), bewigged and reclining, book in hand.

Buried in the churchyard are Ernest Gimson and the Barnsley brothers, Arts and Crafts Movement designers and furniture makers, who made Sapperton their home at the beginning of the 20th

c. *Upper Dowel House*, just beyond the church with fine yew hedges and topiary animals, was built by Ernest Barnsley for himself c. 1901. It was basically formed from two existing cottages, while the high block overlooking the valley was built in imitation cf Daneway House (see below). Beyond this are the houses Ernest Gimson and Sidney Barnsley built themselves – unfortunately Gimson's has been altered, after a fire. Several other houses in the village, and the village hall, were built by Ernest Barnsley. Norman Jewson, the architect, also lived in the village: his house on the village green is easily recognizable from the yew arches and the long-legged topiary bird.

Gimson and the Barnsleys used **Daneway House**, in the valley below, as their workshop and showroom. This lovely old house dates back to the 13th c., when it was a hall house – the original door of the house is still visible, but is now inside. The tall five-storey block, with one room on each floor, was added c. 1620. The two main rooms have original ribbed and decorated plaster ceilings. The house has not been altered since 1717. It can be seen by written appointment; to get there go down into the valley, past *The Daneway Inn*, and it is on the right as the road starts to climb again.

The Daneway Inn, like *The Tunnel House Inn* at Coates, was built for the bargees and professional 'leggers' at the Sapperton end of the 2½m-long canal tunnel. (The 'leggers' were the men who propelled the barges through the tunnel, lying on their backs and using their feet against the tunnel walls.) The archway at the entrance to the tunnel can still be seen, but in places the tunnel has fallen in, and has not been used since 1911.

Pinbury Park, 2m to the NE, stands in a superb position above the beech woods of the Frome valley. The house dates largely from the 17th c., though a medieval building is probably concealed in the main block. Ernest Gimson and the Barnsleys added a wing c. 1900 when they lived here. One of the living rooms has a fine carved stone chimneypiece by Gimson, and one of his characteristic modelled plaster ceilings.

Selsley A4
Village off B4066, 2m SW of Stroud

All Saint's Church is dramatically set on the side of a hill, overlooking Stroud across the valley. Built in 1862, it has probably the earliest set of stained glass by William Morris's firm, Morris & Co. Ford Madox Brown did the Nativity window, Rossetti did the Visitation, and William Morris himself did the Annunciation and the figures of Adam and Eve in the Creation window. The rather extraordinary-looking house next to the church is *Stanley Park*, mainly Victorian with an Elizabethan core.

½m to the S, on Selsley Common, is *The Toots*, a 240ft long barrow resembling two round barrows with a gash in the middle.

Sevenhampton B3/C3
Village off A436, 4½m S of Winchcombe

The village is largely built round a small ford on the infant Coln. The construction of its church, *St Andrew's*, is quite extraordinary. Norman in origin, it was enlarged and enriched in the late 15th c. due to the benefactions of the Worcester wool merchant, John Camber, whose brass is in the church. It was at this period that the Perpendicular central tower was added, supported, amazingly, by flying buttresses within the church, with vaulting high up under the belfry. The N and S transepts and the S porch were added at the same time. The churchyard is most beautifully cultivated as a flower garden.

Seven Springs see *Bisley, Coberley*

Sezincote C2
Historic house off A44, 3m SW of Moreton-in-Marsh

This famous house was built c. 1805 in the Indian style by S.P. Cockerell for his brother Charles, who had amassed a fortune in the service of the East India Company. It has a main block faced with almost orange-coloured stone, an onion-shaped dome, and a long curving greenhouse wing. The Prince Regent's visit to Sezincote c. 1807 undoubtedly inspired the remodelling of the Brighton Pavilion a few years later. The beautifully landscaped *Grounds* were laid out by Humphrey Repton. There is an Indian bridge, surmounted by cast-iron Brahmin bulls, an Indian shrine, and an Oriental water garden.

Slaughters, Lower and Upper C2
Villages off A429/A436, respectively 2m N and 2½m NW of Bourton-on-the-Water

Both these villages lie on the River Eye, a tributary of the Dikler. **Lower Slaughter** is truly picturesque. Here the river is broad and shallow, its banks lined with stone, running under stone footbridges between grassy verges which at one point widen out to form the little village green. Just past the green is the early 19th-c. *Mill*, built of brick, the water wheel still *in situ*. All the buildings in the village are of local stone, with Cotswold stone roofs.

The pleasant church, *St Mary's*, was rebuilt in 1867, except for the N arcade which is restored Transitional Norman. The *Manor House*, now a hotel, was built in 1658 and remained in the hands of the Whitmore family until 1964. Unfortunately, the outside of the house has been much spoilt over the years, but, inside, the dining room has a fine Baroque stone fireplace and a splendid plaster ceiling contemporary with the building of the house. In the grounds is a 16th-c. dovecote, one of the largest in Gloucestershire, and a fine stable block of c. 1770. Despite the enormous number of tourists that come here, the village is well-kept and uncommercialized.

Upper Slaughter, further upstream, though equally impressive, has a less 'tidied-up' look. The village is mainly built on the hillside above the river, and again all the houses are built of locally quarried stone, and still have stone roofs. At the top of the village, with the hills and fields immediately beyond the churchyard, is *St Peter's Church*, originally Norman but much rebuilt in the Middle Ages and later. It has beautiful stone vaulting below the tower, a fine carved Perpendicular font, and many 17th- to 19th-c. monuments and tablets. But the most interesting thing in the church is the *Mortuary Chapel* N of the chancel. This was built by public subscription in 1854 to house the tomb of the Rev Francis Edward Witts, the diarist who was rector here 1808-54 and lord of the manor 1852-4.

The house, now called *The Lords of the Manor Hotel*, a 17th-c. building added to in the 18th and 19th c., was bought by the Rev F.E. Witts in 1852, though the family had lived here long before that. It still belongs to the family and is, incidentally, an excellent place for lunch, with good homemade food and a wonderful outlook, both from inside the house and from the lovely gardens.

On one side of the open square by the churchyard are eight cottages remodelled c. 1906 by Sir Edwin Lutyens. From here two roads lead down to the river, encircling *Castle Mound*, the site of an ancient castle. Finally, there is the old *Manor House*, built on a slope in a superb position overlooking the village and the river below. It is mainly Elizabethan, but the oldest part is a century earlier. The porch is Jacobean.

Sherborne C3/D3
Village off A40, 4½m S of Bourton-on-the-Water

The manor of Sherborne was bought in 1551 by Thomas Dutton, and the Renaissance-style house he built, though demolished and rebuilt in the 19th c., is still very recognisable in the present *Sherborne House*, now converted into flats. Adjacent to it, the *Church of St Mary Magdalene* is actually joined to Sherborne House by a corridor. Rebuilt in the 18th and 19th c., the most interesting things in it are the monuments, including one to Sir John Dutton (1749), by J.M. Rysbrack and another to James Lenox Dutton (1791), by Richard Westmacott the Elder showing a life-sized angel trampling underfoot a prostrate figure of Death.

The E end of the village was completely rebuilt in the early 19th c. as a model village. The cottages are grouped in small terraces with large front gardens. Note the enchanting little *Post Office* with its Victorian frontage and cottage garden.

Snowshill C2
Village off A44, 2½m S of Broadway

For anyone with a tendency to accumulate possessions, a visit to **Snowshill Manor** could be a chastening experience. Charles Wade bought the house in 1919, but he himself lived in the tiny priest's house in the garden, using the house for his magpie collection of almost everything one can think of: roomfuls of cabinets, toys, musical instruments, bicycles and farm carts, suits of armour, dozens of leather fire buckets, dead beetles and butterflies, and so on. Even the cottage where he lived is crammed full of things. He gave the lot to the National Trust, who have left it all just as it was, everything jumbled together, nothing labelled, though many of the items are of considerable interest. The house itself has a seemingly almost unaltered Tudor interior, a S front with three Tudor mullioned and transomed windows and two sash windows dating from c.1700.

The village is built on a steep hill, high, lonely and exposed. The little, old stone cottages cluster not round a green but round the sloping, hummocky churchyard. The small, sturdy *St Barnabas' Church*, completely rebuilt in 1864, is of no great interest, but its setting is perfect, with superb views from the churchyard.

Southrop D3
Village off A417 and A361, 2½m NE of Fairford

A pretty village on the Leach, which is diverted into little streams in the grounds of the manor house, at the bottom of the village. *Southrop Manor* was largely built in the 16th and 17th c., but there seems to have been a late Norman archway near an underground chamber, now sealed off, which is said to have led to the chancel of the church; this was reset into the doorway of the existing dining room in 1926.

Next to the manor house is **St Peter's**

Church. Built *c*.1100, it has some original Norman work, notably the N doorway with its patterned tympanum and a large extent of herringbone masonry in the N and S walls of the nave. There are effigies of a man and his wife in the sanctuary (*c*. 1560), but the church's great treasure is the *font*. Probably *c*.1180, the carving shows figures of armoured women, representing the Virtues, trampling on the opposite Vices; it is worth coming to Southrop just to see this. It is said to have been discovered by John Keble, built into the S doorway. Keble was curate here 1823-5, and it was at his vacation reading parties at the *Old Vicarage* (early 19th-c.) that the first seeds of the Oxford Movement were sown. The village also has some fine farm buildings and a creeper-covered inn called *The Swan*. (See also *Walk 2*, p.19.)

Stanton   C2
Village off A46, 3m SW of Broadway

Situated at the foot of the W scarp, Stanton is a perfect, unspoilt Cotswold village. The buildings date mainly from the 16th and 17th c., and the village seems to have changed little since then – though its appearance today is largely due to the restoration work of the architect Sir Philip Stott, who lived here from 1906 to 1937.

It is worth walking to the top of the village, past the wayside cross (the base is medieval, the shaft 18th-c.) to *The Mount Inn*, where there is a superb view of the Vale of Evesham.

Down in the village is the *Church of St Michael and All Angels*, a 15th-c. rebuilding of a Norman church. The tower, spire, porch and S aisle are Perpendicular: above the porch is a tiny museum of domestic and farm implements. Inside, the three-bay nave arcade is late Norman. Note the 15th-c. font, the wooden boss (from the S aisle's timber roof) now set in the S wall, and the two pulpits, one late 17th-c. and the second, in the N transept, late 14th-c. (no longer used, this is one of the few surviving wooden pulpits of the period).

Stanton Court, built in the 17th c. by the Izod family, was thoroughly restored by Sir Philip Stott. Opposite its gates stands the *Old Manor Farmhouse*, with the inscription '1618' over its doorway. *The Manor* (or *Warren House*) has an even earlier inscription: 'T.W. (for Thomas Warren) 1577.'

Stanway   C2
Village on B4077, 4m NE of Winchcombe

The church, the Tudor manor house and the splendid gatehouse, all faced in golden ashlar, form an exceptionally fine group of buildings. The *Gatehouse*, adjoining the massive garden wall, with its three elaborately shaped gables surmounted by scallop shells, is a much-photographed Cotswold building. Behind it stands **Stanway House**, whose S front, with its four gables and 60-paned oriel window, is best seen from the churchyard. The house was built in the early 17th c. by Sir Paul Tracy in the early Renaissance style: frequently modified, it was restored to its original form, retaining a few later additions, in 1948. The house was one of the last in the country to be built with a great hall: thereafter the owner would eat in a separate room to his servants. In the *Grounds* are many fine specimen trees, an 18th-c. pyramid, and a huge 14th-c. *Tithe Barn*, sometimes used as a hall. Only the garden is open to the public.

A notorious owner of the house was Dr Robert Dover (d. 1742), who as the 'Quicksilver Doctor' dosed his patients with mercury and who, as a privateer in earlier life, captained the ship which rescued Alexander Selkirk (the original Robinson Crusoe) from the island of Juan Fernandez in the Pacific.

St Peter's Church, by the house, was originally Norman but lost most of its original fabric in the Victorian rebuilding. Also in the village is an unusual *war memorial* – an outstanding bronze of St George and the Dragon by Alexander Fisher with lettering by Eric Gill, and a thatched *Cricket Pavilion*, set on staddle stones, which was given to the village by Sir James Barrie, the author, who once lived in Stanway House.

Stow-on-the-Wold D2

Small town at junction of A429/A424/A436, 4m S of Moreton-in-Marsh. Event: Horse Fair (May & Oct). EC Wed. Inf: Tel (0451) 30352

'Stow-on-the-Wold where the wind blows cold' goes the local saying. 700ft above sea level, Stow is the highest town in the Cotswolds. The reason for building a town in such an exposed position is that it is an important road junction: seven major roads meet here, including the Fosse Way. Happily, none of them goes through the centre of the town. Since medieval times Stow has been an important market town, famous for its fairs: on one occasion 20,000 sheep changed hands. Twice a year a horse fair is still held here.

Its position and history are reflected in the lay-out of the town: the buildings are largely grouped round a huge square, which provides shelter from the wind and an enclosed space for the markets and fairs. The huge elm seen in so many pictures of Stow is now sadly gone, but the old stocks can still be seen. As might be expected, there are several old inns in the square, but the most attractive building is *St Edward's House*, early 18th-c. with fluted Corinthian pillars, now a teashop. The market cross is medieval, but its gabled head is Victorian, as is the Town Hall in the centre of the square.

St Edward's Church is in the centre of the town, its four-stage Perpendicular tower dominating the W end of the square. It is Norman in origin, with additions over the centuries. There is a large painting of the Crucifixion attributed to Gaspar de Craeyer, friend of Rubens and Van Dyck, in the S aisle. A thousand Royalists were imprisoned in the church by Cromwell in 1646 after the Battle of Stow.

Stowell Park C3

Historic house off A429, 2m SW of Northleach

The Elizabethan mansion, enlarged and altered by Sir John Belcher at the end of the 19th c., stands in a large park overlooking Chedworth Woods and the Coln valley. It was once the home of the Tames who enlarged Northleach and Rendcomb. Behind the mansion stands *St Leonard's*, a small Norman church, restored in 1898 but otherwise little changed since it was built, except that the top of the original tower collapsed. The most interesting feature is the 12th-c. Doom painting on the N wall of the nave. It shows Our Lady and the Apostles watching the sifting of the souls into the Saved and the Lost.

Stroud A4

Town 13m W of Cirencester, 13m S of Cheltenham. Pop: 19,600. Events: Stroud Show (2nd Sat in Jul), Festival of Religious Drama & the Arts (Oct). EC Thur MD Sat. Inf: Tel (04536) 4252.

The history of Stroud and its early industrial development are reflected in the architecture of the town and the geography of the surrounding country. Rows of undistinguished red brick terraces, built at the end of the last century, huddle along the narrow climbing streets. Stroud is built on steep hills running down into four valleys. Running W to Bristol is the Stroudwater Valley of the River Frome; running E to Cirencester is the Golden Valley, with its steep hillside villages. N of Stroud is the Painswick Valley, and to the S the valley that runs through Nailsworth. From the hills spring the streams which powered the mills of the cloth industry. The natural salts in the spring water made them ideal for cleaning and dyeing the cloth, and Stroud became famous for the scarlet and blue cloth that was used for military uniforms. The Stroudwater Navigation Canal, from Wallbridge to the Severn at Framilode, was opened in 1779 and used for the transport of goods concerned with the industry. There was at that time a network of canals all over England; now, nearly all are abandoned. In the depressions of the 1830s and 1870s the mills began to close. While there were 150 mills working during the height of Stroud's prosperity, by 1979 there were only six working mills in the area.

Much of Stroud has been demolished and rebuilt. Few of the clothiers' houses still stand, though it was once probably a town not unlike Painswick. The important buildings are mainly 19th-c.

The London Road (A419) comes into the centre of the town, dominated by the huge classical façade of the Subscription Rooms; those approaching by the A46 (Nailsworth or Cheltenham) are recommended to use the multistorey car park by the bus station and ascend, via the shopping centre at the upper level, to King Street. From King Street, George Street – opposite the shopping centre – leads to the *Subscription Rooms*. Built in 1833, these rooms are now used for public events and exhibitions. To the left is the *Congregational Chapel* (1837) from which Bedford Street ascends to the High Street.

Turning right up the High Street, the next turning left is *The Shambles*. Originally a meat market, this street has on its E side the Old Town Hall, built *c.* 1594, and on the W an old Victorian market arcade.

St Lawrence's Church, at the top of The Shambles, was rebuilt in 1866-8, retaining only the 14th-c. tower of the original building. Some of the monuments from the old church have been preserved: of particular interest is that to Thomas Stephens (d. 1613), with a kneeling effigy of gilded and painted alabaster. The striking reredos, dated 1872, is by George Gilbert Scott the Younger. There is also some good stained glass, especially that in the N aisle by J.C.N. Bewsey (1913) depicting St George and St Martin.

In Lansdown, N of the church and accessible through the churchyard, is the Stroud Museum, which has archaeological and geological sections and illustrates in detail the history of the cloth industry in Stroud.

2m NE of Stroud is *Slad*, childhood home of Laurie Lee and made famous in his book *Cider with Rosie*.

1m E of Stroud off the A419 is *Nether Lypiatt Manor*, home of Prince and Princess Michael of Kent.

Sudeley Castle   B2/C2
Historic house off A46, ½m SE of Winchcombe

The first castle on this site was built illegally, in the wars between Stephen and Matilda, but the earliest parts of the present building date back to the mid-15th c., when Ralph Boteler, Baron Sudeley, rebuilt the castle.

Boteler's support for the Lancastrian cause in the Wars of the Roses obliged him to surrender the castle to Edward IV. It later passed to Richard III, who added a splendid great hall (since destroyed). Subsequently, the Tudor monarchs made much use of the castle. Catherine of Aragon stayed here, as did Henry VIII and Anne Boleyn. Thomas Seymour, brother of Henry's third queen, Jane, became Lord Seymour of Sudeley: after Henry's death he married Catherine Parr, the King's widow, who lived here for just a year (1547-8) before dying in childbirth. The future Elizabeth I also lived here as a child.

After Seymour's execution (1549) the castle was given to the 1st Lord Chandos. It was held by the 6th Lord Chandos for Charles I in the Civil War, but in 1643 the castle was taken by the Parliamentarians who did much damage and desecrated the chapel. When it was subsequently recaptured by Charles he made it his military headquarters. After the Civil War the castle was partly dismantled to make it inoperable as a fortress.

Much of the existing building is Boteler's castle, including the ruined *Banqueting Hall*, the *Portmore Tower* and the *Tithe Barn*. In the peaceful well-kept grounds is the old Perpendicular chapel (*St Mary's Church*). Restored by Sir George Gilbert Scott, the interior is entirely Victorian, including the lovely marble effigy of Catherine Parr and the canopied tomb.

Sudeley now houses a large collection of toys and dolls, and many items of needlework, furniture, tapestries (the 18th-c. Aubusson bedhangings which belonged to Marie-Antoinette, for example) and paintings, including works by Constable, Turner, Rubens and Van Dyck. In the grounds is a woodland play area and Children's Fortress. At most weekends throughout the summer there are special events: a local craft demonstration, folk dancing, military bands and falconry displays.

Swell, Upper and Lower   C2
Villages respectively 1m NW of Stow-on-the-Wold
(B4077) and 1m W (A436)

In **Upper Swell**, the tiny, mainly Norman *St Mary's Church* stands behind the manor house overlooking the River Dikler, which here flows under an 18th-c. bridge and through an enlarged mill-pond. The 16th-c. *Manor House* has a fine Jacobean two-storey porch and landscaped grounds, but it has an unsuitable modern extension.

Lower or **Nether Swell** is 1m downstream, a village that sprawls along the main road. The little *Church of St Mary the Virgin* stands by the road to Upper Swell. The S aisle and chapel were the nave and chancel of the old Norman church; the present nave and chancel were added in the latter part of the 19th c. The Norman part of the church has a carved tympanum showing the Tree of Life over the S doorway, a small but richly detailed chancel arch and a tiny chancel. The new part has stained glass windows by Clayton and Bell, showing scenes from the Passion, and mural paintings on the chancel walls, also by Clayton and Bell. Nether Swell Manor, now *Hill Place School*, was built by Sir Guy Dawber *c.* 1909-13.

On the road from Upper Swell to Stow, **Abbotswood** is the major work in the Cotswolds of Sir Edwin Lutyens. It was built in 1902 and was the home of the farm tractor millionaire, Harry Ferguson. Lutyens also laid out the exquisite formal *Gardens* whose features include: woodland settings of heathers and rhododendrons, a stream splashing down through a series of pools and waterfalls, a semi-circular pool below a great shell carved out of the wall of the house, and a wrought-iron gate at the bottom of the garden leading straight into the Cotswold hills. The gardens are open some Sundays in spring.

Donnington Fish Farm, near Upper Swell, is open throughout the year.

Swinbrook   D3
Oxfordshire. Village off A40, 2½m E of Burford

An attractive Windrush Valley village, with a rough, sloping green. **St Mary's Church** is exceptionally interesting. Built *c.* 1200, it was enlarged in the 15th c. and has a fine Perpendicular clerestory and windows above the altar, all with clear glass. But what people come to Swinbrook to see are the *Fettiplace Monuments*. Two recesses in the N wall of the chancel, with three shelves in each, contain six members of the family, all reclining stiffly on one elbow. The older three effigies (early 17th-c.) are in stone, the others (late 17th-c., and more life-like) are in marble and alabaster. The church also contains several other monuments to the Fettiplace family; brasses to John Croston and his three wives (died 1470); and 15th-c. misericords on the carved choir stalls.

There are some good 17th- and 18th-c. tombs in the churchyard, where are also buried, side by side, Nancy and Unity Mitford, two of the famous Redesdale daughters. The Redesdales moved here from *Asthall in 1926, and lived at *Swinbrook House*. The mansion in which the Fettiplaces lived was demolished in 1805, when the last Fettiplace died. Down by the river is the picturesque *Swan Inn*, which has a children's room and homemade food.

From the churchyard, a walled path leads to a field and a short cut to the interesting little St Oswald's Church, * *Widford*.

Taynton   D3
Oxfordshire. Village off A424, 1½m NW of Burford

Taynton stone has made this village famous: Blenheim Palace is said to have absorbed 200,000 tons of it; Christopher Wren used it for his London churches, including St Paul's Cathedral; and many of the Oxford colleges and churches are built with it.

Taynton itself is a quiet, attractive village, situated on the side of a hill overlooking the willows and meadows of the Windrush valley. The *Church of St John the Evangelist*, built in the 14th and 15th c., is rich in good stone carving – the corbels on the nave and aisle roofs, the gargoyles, and above all the elaborately carved early 15th-c. font – while the big windows and clerestory make it pleasantly light.

Temple Guiting C2
Village off B4077, 7m W of Stow-on-the-Wold

A secluded village in a beautiful spot among trees down by the River Windrush, Temple Guiting formed part of the property given by Gilbert de Lacy to the Knights Templar in the 12th c. The Knights had a preceptory here, from which they managed their estates.

Little remains of the original 12th-c. *St Mary's Church*. The first major alterations took place in the 15th c., and since then there has been a succession of rebuildings in the style of the day. In the 18th c. the Rev George Talbot put Georgian classical windows in the Perpendicular jambs. *Manor Farm*, one of the finest Cotswold Tudor houses, is 16th-c. To the W of the house is a large dovecote.

1m S is *Kineton*, a hamlet with several 17th-c. cottages and farms.

Tetbury B4
Small town on A433, 10m SW of Cirencester. Event: Woolsack Races (Spring Bank Hol Mon). EC Thur MD alt Wed. Inf: Tel (0666) 53552

Named after Terra, an abbess of Wimborne who founded a monastery here before the Norman Conquest, Tetbury is an attractive market town, with unusually wide streets. Built at the junction of several main roads, it was once an important centre for the wool trade. All roads lead to the Market Place, where stands the splendid 17th-c. *Market House*, supported on three rows of stone pillars. It was probably originally used for weighing wool. Opposite the Market House is *The Snooty Fox*, formerly *The White Hart Hotel*, rebuilt in Jacobean style by Lewis Vulliamy in the mid 19th c.

There are many fine 17th- and 19th-c. houses in the town, evidence of its continuing prosperity as a wool-collecting centre, one of the nearest to the Stroudwater mills. Ultimately the lack of a local water supply, however, prevented Tetbury's industrialization and the transformation of the town on the lines of Nailsworth and Stroud, which had the advantage of water-powered machinery: to this Tetbury owes the preservation of its character.

From the Market House, Church Street leads to the beautiful **St Mary's Church**, well-known as one of the earliest Gothic Revival churches. Built in 1781 it has huge windows and tall, wooden columns supporting the ribbed plaster ceilings. An unusual feature is the passage or ambulatory running along the outside of the aisles and along the W end of the church, with communicating arched doorways. The church also has a gallery with Gothic panelling, straight-backed box pews, and some grandiose monuments.

Returning to the Market House, Chipping Street leads down to *The Chipping*, the original Market Place and now a car park. On its E side at No 5 is a Tudor *Wool Merchant's House* with an old screens passage retaining its original arches. On the N side is *Chipping Steps*, a stepped street of old stone houses.

Long Street, also running from Market House, has many well-preserved 17th- and 19th-c. houses. At the end is the *Old Court House*, which contains the Tourist Information Office and *Police Museum*.

1m SW of Tetbury is *Highgrove House*, home of the Prince and Princess of Wales.

Thames Head see *Coates*

Turkdean C3
Village off A429, 2m N of Northleach

Approached through an avenue of splendid beech trees from the hamlet of Lower Dean to the S, Turkdean itself consists of little more than a church and a few houses and cottages. The originally Norman *All Saints' Church* was largely rebuilt in the 15th c., but on the far side of the church is a small but finely carved Norman doorway reset into the wall. *Rectory Farm* nearby has a 14th- or 15th- c. rib-vaulted undercroft (or crypt) – there is a photo of it in the church.

Uley A4
Village on B4066, 2m E of Dursley

Quite a large village, straggling almost a mile up the hill from Dursley, Uley was once as famous for its blue woollen cloth as Stroud was for its red – the many good Georgian houses in the village are evidence of its former prosperity. At the top of the village stands the Victorian *St Giles's Church*, superbly sited above the road, with fine views from the churchyard, and, just beyond, a small green and *The Old Crown Inn*.

From the church, there is a ½m walk to the Iron Age *Uleybury Hill Fort*, the most spectacular in Gloucestershire. (Remember to take the right fork in the path by the wrought-iron gate of a modern bungalow, and then cross the field at the end of the path). On its huge promontory, with 300ft drops on all sides but the N, this is one of the most impressive prehistoric fortified sites in Britain. The outer rampart of the fort is clearly visible, and it is possible to walk round it (1¼m) with magnificent views in all directions.

Further up the hill, 1m N of Uley, lies the Uley Tumulus, or **Hetty Pegler's Tump**, which, after *Belas Knap*, is the finest long barrow in the Cotswolds. Hetty Pegler was the wife of the man who owned the field at the end of the 17th c. Inside the 120ft-long Neolithic barrow (some 4,500 years old), is a 22ft-long passage, with two pairs of side chambers and one at the end. The chambers are separated by drystone walls and roofed with huge stone slabs. The two on the right have been sealed off, but the others can be explored. The keys to the protective door are available from the cottage on the way up the hill from Uley, which has a notice outside.

Upper Slaughter see *Slaughters*

Upper Swell see *Swells*

Upton House (NT)   D1
Warwickshire. Historic house off A422, 8m N of Banbury

On high ground to the S of Edgehill, this fine mansion was originally built in 1695 for Sir Rushout Cullen, a London merchant. In 1927 the house was bought by the 2nd Viscount Bearsted, largely to house his immense collection of paintings and 18th-c. porcelain. Ex-

tended and remodelled, the house is now mainly 20th-c., and though maintaining much of its original chracter is now more interesting for its contents, and the magnificent gardens and grounds that surround it.

The house contains a set of 16th-c. Brussels tapestries and a good collection of Sèvres porcelain and Chelsea figures. The paintings include outstanding examples of the Continental schools – works by Breughel, Memling, El Greco, Guardi and Canaletto – and English 18th-c. paintings by Stubbs, Hogarth and others.

The terraced *Gardens* descend to a formal lake. There is a water garden, and some way to the E a second lake ornamented by a classical temple built by Sanderson Miller.

Westonbirt Arboretum   B4
Gardens on A433, 3m SW of Tetbury

Westonbirt House, a girls' public school since 1928, was built for R.S. Holford by Lewis Vulliamy in 1863-70, in Elizabethan style; it is Vulliamy's most important surviving domestic building. He was also employed on other buildings on the estate, but *Garden House*, built in what was Holford's nursery garden for the arboretum, was built by Norman Jewson in 1939. The world-famous arboretum is in the grounds of Westonbirt House. Holford began to plant it before 1839: covering 116 acres, it is the best collection of trees in Britain. Rhododendrons, azaleas and camelias make a fine show of colour in spring, while in autumn the brilliant maples – probably the finest collection in the whole of Europe – can be seen.

Whittington   B3
Village off A40, 4m E of Cheltenham

A short distance from the small, compact village, the Norman *St Bartholomew's Church* shelters beneath the high walls of the Elizabethan manor house, *Whittington Court*. The most noticeable thing about the church from the outside is the little wooden bell-turret. Inside, on the floor of the S aisle, are three early 14th-c. stone effigies; two armoured knights and a lady. Note also the headstops on one of the arches separating the nave from the S aisle (the woman is wearing the horned headdress of the 15th c.), and the brass to Richard Cotton (d. 1556) and his wife. It was probably Cotton who started to build the present manor house, which stands on an earlier moated site. (A Roman villa was excavated here in 1952).

Sandywell Park, on the other side of the A40, was built *c.* 1704, and the wings added in 1758.

Widford
D3
Oxfordshire. Village off A40, 1½ m E of Burford

Standing by itself in the middle of a field, only a short walk from Swinbrook, the small *St Oswald's Church* would be worth visiting for its unusual site alone. Built in the 12th and 13th c. on the site of a Roman villa, the church contains fragments of Roman mosaic in the chancel floor, a tub-shaped 13th-c. font, medieval wall paintings and box pews of the late 18th or early 19th c. In 1680 the parish was sold to the Fettiplace family, who also owned Swinbrook. The church was restored in1904, having been abandoned in the middle of the previous century. Around the church, much evidence has been found of a deserted medieval village.

Willersey
C2
Village on A46, 1½ m N of Broadway

Situated at the foot of the Cotswold Scarp but described by H.J. Massingham in *Wold Without End* as 'proper Cotswold', Willersey has wide greens on either side of the road; a duckpond by which stands the charming 17th-c. *Pool House*, with its imposing stone gate-piers; the pleasant-looking *Bell Inn*; and a medieval church, *St Peter's*, with a big Perpendicular central tower complete with buttresses, embattled parapet, pinnacles and gargoyles. The lovely vaulting under the tower is Victorian, but the massive pillars supporting it were designed by Abbot Zattan of Evesham (d. 1418). Willersey used to be the summer residence of the Abbots of Evesham. The only thing that spoils this idyllic village is the busy A46, which runs through it.

Winchcombe
B2
Small town on A46, 7m NE of Cheltenham. EC Thur

The history of Winchcombe goes back over 1000 years. The Benedictine Abbey was founded *c.* 798 by King Kenulf of Mercia, and the town grew up around it. Kenulf's young son Kenelm was said to have been murdered by his sister, Quendrida, and the Abbey became an important pilgrimage centre as the resting place of the martyred St Kenelm. Two stone coffins found on the Abbey site and now to be seen in Winchcombe church are said to be those of Kenulf and Kenelm. After the Dissolution in 1539, the Abbey was totally destroyed by Lord Seymour of Sudeley.

Despite a small clothing trade and the brief emergence of a tobacco-growing industry in the 16th and early 17th c., the town declined dramatically after the Dissolution. It seems that it had depended almost entirely on the pilgrim trade for its prosperity. In 1640 it was described as a 'poor, beggarly town'.

Today, Winchcombe is an attractive, lively little town, with houses closely packed together along its main streets. The fine Perpendicular **St Peter's Church** was built *c.*1465, a joint venture of town and Abbey. Outside, the embattled parapets on nave, aisles and porch, the magnificent gilded weathercock, and the 40 gargoyles (thought to be caricatures of local worthies) make a memorable sight. (The bullet marks on the tower and elsewhere are a legacy of Civil War battles.) Inside, the church is light and spacious: it has 16 clerestory windows on each side, all with pale greenish glass, and no chancel arch. Only a 15th-c. oak screen separates nave from chancel – note the little imp near the pulpit. The altar cloth framed on the N wall is made out of late 14th-c. priests' copes and is said to be the work of Catherine of Aragon, whose pomegranate emblem is embroidered round the hem. The tomb of Thomas Williams of Corndean (d. 1636) in the chancel should not be missed: the kneeling effigy in painted stone looks at the empty space left for his wife, who remarried and was buried with her second husband.

Opposite the church in Queen Square is *Jacobean House* (1619). Attributed to Inigo Jones, the building was restored by the Dent family of Sudeley in 1876. Nearby are the *Chandos Almshouses* (1573) built by the Chandos family who were lords of the manor at Sudeley Castle in the Elizabethan and Stuart periods.

To the E of Queen Square, *Vineyard Street* has a delightful row of cottages running down to the River Isbourne. This was once known as Duck Street, because it was here that witches and 'scolds' used to be ducked.

NE from Queen Square, Abbey Terrace leads past the *Abbey Site* to the High Street. Here is the Town Hall, with the old stocks outside and inside a *Museum* of local history. Opposite is the galleried *George Inn* (16th-c.) which was a hostel for pilgrims to the Abbey.

The *Winchcombe Railway Museum*, 100yds W of the church at No.23 Gloucester Street, is well worth a visit, though open only on Bank Holidays and in early August.

1m N of Winchcombe on the A46, a turning left for Greet leads to *Winchcombe Pottery*, where there is a little shop adjoining the potters' workshops. 1m further N at Toddington is the *GWR (Gloucestershire Warwickshire Railway) Exhibition*, a restored section of a derelict line with a station, signal box and buffet car serving snacks. This is the project of the Cheltenham and Stratford Railway Association, whose object is to restore some old steam locomotives and reopen sections of the former Great Western Railway line between the two towns.

½m SE of Winchcombe is **Sudeley Castle*, and 2m to the S **Belas Knap*.

Windrush
D3
Village off A40, 4½ m W of Burford

The village lies on a hillside just S of the point where the River Sherborne runs into the Windrush. There are weirs and a lovely old mill, and houses and cottages grouped round the small triangular green – all built of the particularly good local stone. *St Peter's Church* has a Norman S doorway, with a double row of grotesque beakheads. Inside, the roof timbers of the nave rest on reset 12th-c. grotesque corbel heads: look out for the sheep's head corbel above the aisle arcade. The tower is Perpendicular, and the splendid carved pulpit, Jacobean. The churchyard contains a magnificent group of 18th-c. table-tombs.

Withington
C3
Village off A436 and A40, 4m W of Northleach

An attractive village near the head of the Coln Valley, with good stone cottages, a 16th-17th-c. gabled *Manor House* and dovecote, a pleasant 18th-c. *Rectory* and an interesting church, *St Michael's*. The church has Norman doorways – a particularly elaborate one on the S – and fine Perpendicular clerestory windows. Inside, the walls have unfortunately been scraped, but the Howe monument (1651), showing Sir John, Lady Howe and their eight children is worth seeing. They all lived at *Cassey Compton*, a 17th-c. mansion 1m E of Withington. *The Mill Inn* is an interesting old inn with a large garden on the mill stream.

Woodchester
A4
Village on A46, 1½m S of Stroud

Situated on the steep W slopes of the Avon Valley, with old mills at the valley bottom and some good clothiers' houses on the slopes, Woodchester is known for its magnificent **Roman Pavement**, almost 50ft square, discovered here by Samuel Lysons of Rodmarton in the late 18th c. The mosaic shows Orpheus charming the birds and beasts with the music of his lyre. Lysons' excavations exposed a villa of sixty rooms, all in the churchyard of the abandoned St Mary's Church. Little now remains of the church, and nothing above ground of the villa. The mosaic itself is kept covered with earth to preserve it, and until now had been exposed only once every ten years. The last time was in 1973, but it seems that it may never be uncovered again because of the damage it suffers.

To reach the churchyard, take the turning for North Woodchester, drive to the top of the hill and turn right down a no-through road. A good idea of what the pavement would have been like can be obtained from the Wotton Mosaic at *Wotton-under-Edge*, where a minutely detailed reconstruction of the mosaic has almost been completed.

The present *St Mary's Church* is a mid-19th-c. building by S.S. Teulon. Another mid-19th-c. construction, ranked by David Verey as 'one of the great achievements of 19th-c. domestic architecture in England' is *Woodchester Park*, built for Lord Ducie by Benjamin Bucknall, a friend of Viollet-le-Due (3m to the SW).

Wotton-under-Edge A4

Small town on B4508, 5½m S of Dursley. EC Thur MD Fri

Built right on the edge of the W escarpment above the Severn Vale, the first record of the town (then *Wudetun*, Saxon for 'farm in the wood') dates from a royal charter of 940AD. The old village was burnt to the ground in the reign of King John, but, after it was rebuilt, it became one of the most important Cotswold wool and clothing towns. Flemish weavers came here in the 14th c., and, in the 17th and 18th c., mills were built by the stream and many of the cottages had a third storey added to house a loom. Katharine, Lady Berkeley, founded Wotton Grammar School in 1384. One of the earliest schools in the country, it is now a flourishing comprehensive (but on a different site). Edward Jenner, pioneer of vaccination, was one of its pupils. Another famous resident was Isaac Pitman, who was teaching in Wotton in 1837 when he invented his system of shorthand. His house in Orchard Street is marked by a plaque.

There are several buildings of interest in Wotton. The *Tolsey*, on the corner of the High Street and Market Street, a 17th-c. building with a conical roof and dragon weather-vane, once used to house the Court of Pie Powder (set up to deal with offences concerning the travelling traders – those with 'pied poudre' or 'dusty feet'). *Market Street*, leading to the old market place or *Chipping*, has many 16th-c. timbered houses and the *Town Hall*, originally built as a covered market in 1698.

Berkeley House, at No.31 Long Street, is a fine 17th-c. Jacobean house, from which a whole room, with pine panelling painted green and 18th-c. Chinese wallpaper, was sold to the Victoria and Albert Museum in 1924 (an earlier oak-panelled room was sold to an American museum). In Church Street, at the end of Long Street, are the *Perry Almshouses* (1638) which have their own chapel and face onto a little courtyard on the other side of which are the *Dawes Almshouses* of 1720 and the General Hospital.

From the N end of Church Street, the Cloud leads to the **Church of St Mary the Virgin**. Originally 13th-c., this large, light church is a 15th-c. rebuilding with a magnificent Perpendicular tower, wide spacious aisles, and clerestory. Its walls are covered with 17th-19th-c. monuments, but the church's great treasure, in the N aisle, is the *Tomb of Thomas Lord Berkeley*, the lord of the manor, and his wife Margaret. It is thought to date from 1392, and its life-sized brasses are among the oldest and most beautiful in the country. Thomas Berkeley, who served Henry IV as an Admiral of the Fleet and fought with Henry V at Agincourt, is shown with a delightful curly-maned lion at his feet: his wife has a little dog at hers. (Replicas of the brasses are available for rubbing.) The church organ, originally given to St Martin's-in-the-Fields in London by George I in 1726, and played by Handel, was bought by the vicar of Wotton in 1799.

At Rowland Hill's *Tabernacle*, high up on the hill, is the *Wotton Mosaic*, a meticulous reconstruction of the famous *Woodchester Roman Pavement, now almost complete.

1m NW of Wotton, just E of the B4060, in the middle of Westridge Wood, are the *Brackenbury Ditches*, the remains of an Iron Age hill fort.

Index